4/6/21
To Jun !
with my blessings
Dr. Dom

Never
Too Late

Dr. Dom Contreras, Ph.D.

Express Press, Lima, Ohio

NEVER TOO LATE

REPRINT 2004

FIRST EDITION
Copyright © 2002 by
Dr. Dominic Contreras, Ph.D.

Library of Congress Catalog Card Number: 2001-126897

Scripture references are taken from the *New American Standard Bible*, © 1960, 1962, 1963, 1968, 1971, 1972, 1973, 1975, 1977 by The Lockman Foundation. Used by permission.

ISBN 0-7880-2050-1
                PRINTED IN U.S.A.

Introduction

I have endeavored to share in the following pages some of my personal experiences as a pastor and chaplain. I have tried to describe how people deal with their emotions when they are faced with a crisis, trauma or a death in their lives. These are real life experiences that have impacted and helped comfort others in their time of trial.

My hope is that my experiences will help others when they are faced with a crisis to be better equipped to live through the ordeal. Paul the apostle wrote in his letter to the Philippians that through his trials, he had learned to be content. The scripture states, "Not that I speak from want; for I have learned to be content in whatever circumstances I am." (Philippians 4:12). Paul's entire life as a believer was spent serving the Lord. He suffered great deprivations for his religious beliefs. He had learned how to be content in all of life's circumstances. All of us must go through the trials of life as a learning process.

I also pray that my experiences will bring insight on how to minister to those who are going through a trial, or who are grieving over the loss of a loved one. My hope is that what I have learned in ministry will encourage young men and women who are starting out in ministry to not despair, but trust in the Lord for their guidance in ministering to those who are suffering.

It is my profound desire that those who pick up this book will grow spiritually from my life's journey.

Each incident is part of my life. Each individual I have written about has dramatically effected me. These are real individuals with feelings and emotions. Because of laws of privacy, I have endeavored to protect their identities.

As you read, you will feel much of the pain that I personally experienced. Some of the situations and incidents I have described will be very graphic. I want to thank the nurses, physicians and friends who inspired me to put my life experiences in writing. I want to thank my wife for being there for me in all my writing endeavors.

I owe a great debt of thanks and tremendous admiration for the editing of the book to Dr. Harold Helms who patiently read and edited the final copy. I am truly blessed of God for his help and support.

First and foremost I want to thank the good Lord for His inspiration and the leading I have received through the Scriptures.

Chapter One

Genesis

Beep, beep, beep is all I can hear. It's not a steady beat, but inconsistent, and it sounds as if it wants to stop. It is the unsteady rhythm of an erratic heart. I glance at the heart monitor and am entranced by the constant beep. But I'm also wondering if the heart will stop completely. It then dawns on me that the uneven, extremely slow heart rate is my own. The realization sinks in; I am in serious trouble.

I've been admitted to the intensive care unit of Natividad Medical Center. I don't panic, yet I am in a state of shock as to what is transpiring. Am I going to die? Is there a cure? I don't have a clue. All I know is that they are running all sorts of analysis of my blood and have asked a multitude of questions about my physical history. This is my second experience at being a patient confined to an intensive care unit; two years prior I had major surgery for prostate cancer and spent four days in intensive care.

This stay in the Intensive Care unit would last a total of five days and my entire stay at the hospital would be eleven days. When I left the hospital I had a new perspective on life and am still amazed at how God works in our lives.

Being in an intensive care unit can give you a different purview on life and how fragile we truly are. And how much we truly need Christ in our lives to give us His peace and strength. As a Christian it drew me closer to Him, as it made me more aware of His presence in my life.

One night I was unable to sleep. I glanced at the clock, as I was channel surfing on the television, the clock said it was two in the morning. When you are unable to get out of bed and your room is across from the nurse's station, you are not going to get much sleep. Besides, there was the constant sound of an unsteady beat of a heart that is not functioning as it was designed. My mental state and my emotions were frazzled. My thoughts focused on my wife and what would happen to her, should Jesus call me home.

I decided to pray and ask God for His peace and direction for our ministry. I also prayed if He wanted us to stay in our present assignment. Our church has a small congregation and we had been seeking the Lord's will about leaving. I prayed, "Lord, if You want us to stay in the Salinas Valley and continue in our present capacity as pastor of Light of the Valley Christian Fellowship, then open doors for me to minister in this hospital." It was strange that I would pray in such a manner. God had placed a burden on my heart that was to drastically change my life and impact my outlook on life and ministry. A few days later I was moved to the medical surgical ward until a final decision was made as to how they were going to treat my condition.

This particular hospital is a teaching hospital with 21 resident doctors in a three- year residency program. It graduates seven residents every year and receives seven new ones. The chief internist, Dr. Slack, came into my room along with some of the residents. He asked how I was getting along, as he examined my vitals we exchanged pleasantries. Then came the question that changed my life. He stated to me that he and the other doctors in the hospital had been talking about me. They knew I was a minister and were impressed with my concern for the other patients. He asked if I would be interested in being the spiritual leader of the hospital, the chaplain. I could not contain my laughter and explained to Him concerning the prayer I had prayed when I was in the intensive care unit. God had answered my prayer, His plan for my life was revealed.

My answer to the physician was, without hesitation, an affirmative yes. God had spoken through this doctor and showed His will for my life. I knew without a doubt that the Lord had called me to this vital ministry. Reflecting back, I was reminded what Paul the Apostle wrote, "But I want you to know, brethren, that the things which happened to me, have actually turned out for the furtherance of the gospel" (Phil. 1:12). This verse of Scripture brings comfort in knowing that God can make all things work together for His glory.

While I was a patient, I became acquainted with many of the staff, nurses and doctors. Some of the patients found out that I was a minister and came to my room, asking me to pray for them. In December of 1994 I officially became the chaplain of Natividad Medical Center. I am on call 24 hours a day for emergency life-threatening situations, and crisis intervention. I maintain office hour's three days a week, and make normal rounds when I am in the hospital. Part of my ministry is visiting and praying for patients and the medical staff and other employees. I also am available for grief counseling and other issues pertaining to ministry. I have also performed weddings and officiated at funerals for employees and patients.

My heart problem turned out to be a genetic problem and is controlled with medication, diet and healthy exercise. A pacemaker was implanted that is calibrated every three months. I was placed on a low fat, low salt, low cholesterol diet and advised to continue to exercise daily.

Far too many people with various types of afflictions believe that medicine has a cure for all forms of illness. They think that all they have to do is ingest a magic pill and they will be cured: when in reality a change of life style is needed.

I first started having problems with my erratic heart rate in 1992, shortly after we accepted the pastorate in a small community called Chualar, California, which is located approximately 10 miles south of the city of Salinas, in the heart of the Salinas Valley. It has a small population, around 750 inhabitants. The name Chualar comes from a Spanish name meaning, "pig-weed."

At times the residents may feel that they are in a farming community in Old Mexico. We have a grammar school, K through eighth grade, a rural fire department and a post office. There are also three or four grocery stores that meets the needs of the local populace. The population is made up of mostly Mexican Nationals that work the rich farming lands of the Salinas Valley. If you are not Spanish speaking, you are at a loss. This little colony goes back to the days of the Spaniards and was originally a large pig farming community.

The final analysis stated that my heart condition was a congenital defect that was passed on to me by my mother.

Early Recollections

While I was in the hospital and at home recuperating, I prayed and meditated on what had happened to me, where I was going in ministry, how I could use my life experiences, in helping others. I also thought of the many sicknesses and hospitalizations I had incurred over the years.

My first surgery was when I was nine years old, the removal of my tonsils. As a nine-year-old, I was a terror to my siblings, being the fourth child of nine and the first boy. You can understand how spoiled I was. To make matters worse, I was a sickly child. The plan was to remove my tonsils along with my adenoids. Much to my disappointment, it was supposed to make me get over the colds that I constantly caught unfortunately it didn't.

I remember I fought all the way to the hospital and to this day I do not believe these oval masses should be removed from the human anatomy. We are born with tonsils, given to us for a purpose by God. They help fight infection and diseases and people do very nicely with them intact. In those days, the consensus was that if they were infected, you removed them. Not so today, they remove them only as a last resort.

The Good Samaritan

The first time I was hospitalized for any length of time was shortly after my tonsillectomy. Being one of nine children I was the only one that was stricken with scarlet fever. In the 1930s it was not just a matter of taking penicillin; there was no such drug. Scarlet fever was highly contagious and life threatening. I was hallucinating due to an extremely high fever. My mother was frantic and felt trapped with nowhere to turn. Phones, in those days for most, were a luxury and since we did not have a phone, she felt hopeless, as to how to get help. At this time my father was out looking for a job and if he did find work, it paid a dollar a day.

The year was 1939 and the depression was at it's worst. We lived in a two bedroom upstairs apartment with my grandmother, my parents and five other brothers and sisters. My mother had to get me to the hospital or I would have died.

We had a neighbor who happened to have a car. He truly exemplified the teachings of Christ, "Love your neighbor as yourself." A young man in his early to mid twenties. He was from a large African American family. He truly was a Good Samaritan; his intervention saved my life. He drove through the streets of Los Angeles to White Memorial Hospital, in East Los Angeles. Today, it is called L.A. General. He was driving at great speed, with my mother in the back seat holding me on her lap.

When we arrived at the hospital, they took us to the old part of the facility, the county poverty ward. Practically everyone was on government aid; called the W.P.A. In those days they didn't have a children's ward in most county hospitals. Because I had a highly contagious disease and was a Mexican American, I was placed in a bed next to an inmate who was chained to the bed. I was frightened beyond anything that I had encountered in my young life. All the time I was in fear of what they were going to do to me.

Even today that memory is painful. But here I am, almost 60 years later, and I survived. As I look back I am amazed how resilient we are as humans. It is my conviction that God supernaturally intervened in saving my life.

My emotional state became a prison for me. The man who was chained in the bed next to me later turned out to be a comfort to me. He talked to me and consoled me when I cried and helped me through a very traumatic time in my young life. I never forgot his kindness. This man was a prisoner in his circumstances only, but free in his ability to comfort a frightened child. I don't know if this man was a believer or not, but I know God used him to comfort me and used his circumstances to teach me one of life's principles. Regardless of our circumstances, Jesus is always with us in our time of need.

The Apostle Paul was imprisoned numerous times, however he used his circumstances to witness to the other prisoners. While incarcerated he also wrote many of his epistles. Rather than complain about his circumstances, he used them to glorify God.

When I came home from the hospital I found a sign hung on the door stating that we were not allowed to leave the premises. In my young mind I felt we had become prisoners of the County Board

9

of Health; they had quarantined our home. The only one who was allowed to leave the house was my father, to go to work. I was recovering from a highly contagious disease, yet not a single other family member contacted the disease. God had intervened in a way that we could not comprehend. As far as I am concerned it was God who healed me, and it was God who used it for His glory.

Actually God was preparing me for ministry even then, so that at a future date I would glorify Him. "But I want you to know, brethren, that the things which happened to me have actually turned out for the furtherance of the gospel" (Phil. 1:12). I now see how He used this as a learning experience for me that would help me in ministry years later.

Chapter Two

Remember The Prisoners

One of the ministries that I have been privileged to do is ministering to inmates who are incarcerated. Early in our ministry, we were blessed to start a church in Susanville, California, a small town 90 miles north of Reno, Nevada. This community of approximately 9,000 inhabitants is located on the eastern side of the Sierra Nevada Mountains. There the Lord opened doors for me to become a part time prison chaplain. It is difficult to describe the intense environment, the explosive mental frame of mind that these men have to deal with on a daily basis.

When Jesus was crucified, He was hung between two criminals: "Then one of the criminals who were hanged blasphemed Him, saying if you are the Christ, save Yourself and us, But the other, answering, rebuked him, saying 'Do you not even fear God, seeing you are under the same condemnation? And we indeed justly, for we receive the due reward of our deeds; but this Man has done nothing wrong.' Then he said to Jesus, "Lord remember me when You come into Your kingdom," And Jesus said to him, "Assuredly, I say to you, today you will be with Me in Paradise," (Luke 23:39-43). This passage of scripture has been a blessing when I have ministered to inmates. The thief on the cross; tried to comfort our Lord, and he was rewarded with eternal salvation. He knew that he was guilty, but his belief saved him.

We spent seven years in Susanville establishing a healthy, viable church. Six and a half years were also spent in ministering to inmates and, in many instances to their wives and families. Many of the wives of the inmates who were incarcerated became members of our church.

Susanville will always be a place of many wonderful memories and the impact it made on us personally. Only the Lord can measure how we benefited and how we influenced others lives.

Part of my current function as a chaplain is praying and ministering to inmates who are incarcerated by the State of California at Soledad Prison, about 20 miles south of Salinas. There are two prisons at this location: one is a level one and two institution, reserved for less violent inmates. Level three and four is for the most violent men whose chances of going back into society and becoming productive citizens is slim. Their crimes are of a more heinous nature.

Since Natividad hospital is a county hospital, part of its funding comes from the state. Thus it is contracted to care for inmates who need to be hospitalized. Each one of these men is chained to the bed. Each prisoner has two officers guarding him around the clock. I have ministered to those who are dying and those who will recover. I have prayed for men who were serving life imprisonment, as well as men who were full term AIDS patients. I have also prayed for pedophiles, child molesters, men who are considered pariahs to society.

A couple of years ago an inmate was admitted to the intensive care unit, due to an altercation with other prisoners. The other inmates had found out that he was a child molester (when you are a known pedophile, your chances of surviving in prison are very slim). The other inmates gave him a "Colombian Necktie". In other words, they slit his throat and tried to pull his tongue through the gash in his neck. The hostility of the environment, plus the prisoner code, would not allow this man to be incarcerated within the general population.

All pedophiles are generally separated from the other inmates, for the express purpose of protecting them from the other felons. This man was in critical condition and his prognosis was not good. He would remain in the intensive care unit for several weeks.

Since I am required by the hospital administration to document my contact with the patients, I have access to charts and documents. When I read this man's chart and spoke with officers, my assumptions were correct. They confirmed my suspicions. It is a violent society and each convict understands the self-imposed prisoner code.

12

Pedophiles are called "Chesters," from the term "Chester the Molester." Once you wear this label you are marked for life. While this man was a patient I was able to visit and pray for him. It was my understanding that he came to know Christ as his personal Savior. It seemed he was on his way to recovery. He was later transferred to the Medical Surgical ward. The irony of it all, he died of a heart attack within a few days while still in the hospital.

Most people have an aversion for such human beings. Maybe this was God's way of swift justice. But I feel He gave this man time to repent, then took him home.

When I think about this man's life, I often think about the emotional state of mind that these men have to live by each day of their lives. Living in constant fear that they will be exposed as a child molester. All it takes is a whisper by an inmate or a guard to another and the vendetta will be carried out. These men live in constant fear of death in an environment that does not allow for open emotions, not being able to cry or to share your fears openly. They live totally within themselves.

The victims whom this man had molested would most likely shout for joy. How tragic it is that we as Christians get caught up in the hysteria of retribution. These men or women should not go unpunished for their crimes against innocent victims. They deserve every judgment that the law allows. But we must be compassionate as to their eternal salvation.

Sexual molestation is a learned behavior. In all my years of counseling people, and having spent time counseling pedophiles, most were molested themselves. Based on what they have shared with me, they learned this due to their own exploitation by a family member or close family friend. When they go into detail about their own experiences as well as their assault upon a young child, it is extremely difficult to be objective and forgiving. Society states that there is no known cure for this aberrant behavior. Only a loving God our Lord Jesus Christ can deliver a person from such bondage. Paul the apostle addressed certain types of behavior as sin and mentions that they were delivered from this bondage, "And such were some of you; but you were washed, but you were sanctified, but you were justified in the name of the Lord Jesus Christ" (1Cor. 6:9-11).

As I reflect back over the years of my early childhood and remember the incident of my first confinement to a hospital, I can still feel the despair of being in a strange environment. The feeling of loneliness, yet being comforted by a man in the bed next to me, a man in chains. I can empathize with all inmates regardless of why they are imprisoned. God can take a page in our lives, a moment in time, and use it for His glory.

"Remember the prisoners as though in prison with them" (Heb. 13:3a). All life is precious to God. Regardless of our station in life, He loves all sinners. Far too many people judge men and women who are incarcerated as beyond help. They also need Christ in their lives. Perhaps if they had been told about Jesus at an early age, they could have been spared the life that contributed to their fall. I have seen men and women who gave their hearts to Christ simply because someone remembered them.

Chapter Three

Make You Fishers Of Men

While at home recuperating, I thought back to my conversion and early years of ministry. My mind focused on what would have happened to me if Christ had not come into my life?

I remember the joy I felt when I realized that He would guide my life. I also wondered what type of ministry God would place us in?

Prior to being called into the ministry full time, I spent twenty years in retail sales. Twelve of those years were spent in middle management in an executive capacity for a major retail chain. The last four years of the twenty were as a store manager in Medford, Oregon.

I started out my young adult life as a professional baseball player with the Chicago Cub's organization. The Korean War shortened my career and when I returned from the Army I developed shoulder problems. Being a pitcher with a sore arm will not get you very far in baseball when you are trying to establish yourself. I was a power pitcher with a super fast ball and a tremendous curve. I had all the natural ability a person could desire, but I lacked one thing, a personal commitment to a personal God. I might add that no one ever told me that Jesus died for my sins until I was over forty years of age. God had to take us to Medford, Oregon before I came into a personal relationship with my Lord and Savior Jesus Christ.

My life was very empty, not having a clue what salvation meant. I was raised in a cold Roman Catholic, non-church attending family. I had gone through some personal setbacks. I was searching for something to fill the void. Through a process of what I thought was a coincidence, I met a local pastor while playing a round of golf at a local golf course in Medford, Oregon. And I kept meeting this fellow in some of the strangest circumstances and places.

One day while reading the local newspaper, my eye observed a small article concerning Mark Hatfield; Republican senator for the state of Oregon. Having a keen interest in politics and wanting to hear what he had to say about national politics, I told my wife it would be nice to hear him speak.

The evening arrived for us to attend the meeting, held at one of the local high schools. I was not prepared for what awaited us. When we arrived at the school, I noticed all the people had Bibles in their hands and the first person to greet me was the pastor I was continually running into. I glanced at my wife and asked her if we should leave or stay. We selected the latter, a decision that would dramatically change our lives. It turned out that this meeting was a Full Gospel Businessmen's Fellowship International monthly gathering.

Through a process of accepting an invitation to have coffee after the meeting with Pastor Gary and his lovely wife, Judy, and another couple, Jack and Lynda, (the church's assistant pastors), I invited both couples to our home for dinner the next week. I offered to prepare a home-cooked Mexican meal. Gary and Judy were the only ones who were able to come to our home. Saturday evening arrived and I had cooked my specialty, Chile Verde, with all the Mexican food trappings, rice, beans and tortillas. Not wanting to embarrass our guests, we dispensed with the wine.

As the evening came to a close, Gary asked if he could pray for my wife and me, and our home. Not wanting to sound disrespectful, I said it was ok. While he was praying I thought how nice it was to have someone pray for you and your home. It was the first time anyone had ever prayed in my home as a blessing. At the close of his prayer I asked them where their church was located and what time the services started. I said, "You have come to my house: we will come to your house of worship." We could not attend the following day, but we would attend the subsequent Sunday.

Sunday came with much anticipation. We drove to the church and were greeted by exceptionally warm and friendly people. This was our first impression of our future spiritual home. I thought to myself, "Are all Christians as warm and friendly?" It was my first contact with what in the past, I had called "Holy Rollers." I still remember the songs of praise and worship; it was a feeling of euphoria that I had never before experienced. It reached to the core of my soul preparing me for the next phase of the service.

I cannot tell you what was said from the pulpit. But when Gary asked if there were those who wanted to ask Christ into their hearts, I remember I was one of those who stood. A passion for God was instilled in my heart. I recall the placing of hands on my shoulders by another person in the congregation. I felt warm all over, as if all the sins, all the bad judgements in my life, had been washed away. The mistakes and choices that had impacted others had been wiped clean. I was born again.

Our life as members of Faith Bible Center, the Foursquare church in Medford, Oregon, started that day and dramatically changed, our lives. We found ourselves trying to quench a hunger in our souls for the things of God that has never waned. I still have a deep passionate desire for His Word.

We reflect back at these times and even today, we yearn for those early days, of our Christian walk. We established friendships that are very dear to us until this day, relationships that were cemented by the blood of Christ.

Before I Formed You

In the spring of 1976 we purchased a new car in order to go on vacation. Our plan was to go to Glacier National Park, then to Boise, Idaho to a Full Gospel Businessman's convention.

Part of our vacation plan was that we would spend time in Sand Point, Idaho. We found and rented a small "A frame" cabin for several days. We truly enjoyed the majestic splendor of Lake Pend Oreille and the small community. One morning as we were eating breakfast, all of a sudden I began to weep. Tears were streaming down my cheeks. It was so clear; God was speaking to my heart. He said He was calling us into full time ministry. Tricia asked me what was wrong? My answer was that the Lord had spoken to me about us going into full time ministry. Her response was God's way of confirmation; she stated that the Lord had spoken to her that same morning.

17

God does not call only one person in the marriage into ministry. He calls both husband and wife. There has to be unity in the marriage in order for the ministry to succeed. If the pair is not in agreement, they will fail. We were excited and elated; knowing God had a special plan for our lives.

We continued our trip and found ourselves in Boise, Idaho a week later at the Full Gospel convention. At one of the morning sessions, an elderly gentleman brought a prophecy, which I felt, was directed to me personally. I could only see the back of his head, but I instinctively knew that God was speaking. He confirmed that we had been set apart for full time ministry. After spending a lot of time in prayer and conversation, we continued to wait on God for further confirmation. The Bible states, "Every fact is to be confirmed by the testimony of two or three witnesses" (II Cor. 13:1).

Arriving home I contacted my mother. I had two questions on my heart: first, had she ever been in Angeles Temple, and second, was my father a believer? She stated that as far as she knew, my father believed in God. I later led my Dad to a saving relationship with our Lord Jesus Christ.

Concerning Angeles Temple, she stated, as a matter of fact, she had. I had been born a block from Angeles Temple. When she was pregnant with me, our family was going hungry. There was scarcely any food in the house and hardly a prospect of a job for my father. The year was 1930, deep in the throes of the worst depression the world has ever known. Life was extremely bleak. She had sought help at various places, such as the Red Cross, the Catholic Church and other agencies. She then remembered that Aimee Semple McPherson had a radio program and that Sister Aimee would invite the poor and the hungry to come for food and clothing.

Mother went to Angeles Temple expecting to be turned down again. Instead, she was given food and cloth for baby diapers, as well as other needful things for a new baby. Sister Aimee prayed for her and dedicated the baby in her womb to Jesus, in hopes that someday the baby would serve the Lord in ministry.

When I heard the last part of the saga, I dropped the phone and started rejoicing. You see, somehow deep inside I knew, I had been set apart to serve the Lord while I was still in my mother's womb.

As she continued with the account, I was reminded of what our Lord taught about feeding the poor and giving shelter to the needy.

There are studies being done on the bonding process that takes place while the baby is still in the mother's womb. Scripture also confirms that a baby felt the emotions and the presence of another. Luke tells us, "And it happened, when Elizabeth heard the greeting of Mary, that the babe leaped in her womb; and Elizabeth was filled with the Holy Spirit" (Luke 1:41). Paul the Apostle states that, God "had set me apart, even from my mother's womb" (Gal. 1:15). Jeremiah the prophet was told by God, "Before I formed you in the womb I knew you, And before you were born I consecrated you; I have appointed you a prophet to the nations" (Jer. 1:5).

There are Biblical principles that some Christian denomination's practice. One is called "the Laying on of Hands" when praying and dedicating a baby, or praying for the sick. The Laying on of Hands and dedicating a baby while it is still in the womb is extremely important in God's plan for our lives. I believe the life that is being formed can feel and sense emotions; remember the baby has a soul, and the soul consists of the mind, emotions, and will. When my mother related her experience I instinctively knew that this action in my life had taken place. I then asked my mother, why she had never related this? To my amazement she had no answer. In retrospect I realized that God had a plan for my life and it was He who held her back from relating this story. Otherwise, I would not have experienced such joy and adulation as I felt that day. It still remains clear in my mind and is embedded deeply in my heart.

In the Mouth of Two or Three

We had been home from our vacation for about six weeks and our church was having a family camp outside of Medford in the nearby mountains. Tricia and I were able to arrange our busy schedules to fit the camp dates so we could attend.

We arrived at the campsite, and were awed by the splendor of the forest and the smell of fresh pine. The second day we were in camp while pitching horseshoes, a young man approached me. He introduced himself to me and stated that he was from the Eugene,

Oregon, Foursquare Church, where he served as youth pastor. He informed me that while he was pitching horseshoes, God had spoken to him and that he was to tell me that God had called me into full time ministry.

To this day I am completely baffled at the way the Lord calls people to a life of service. I don't recall the young brother's name, but I thank the good Lord that he was obedient to what God had spoken to him concerning me. However I was reluctant to share this incident with the pastoral staff of our church.

A few weeks later we were invited to a gathering to hear an evangelist at a fellow brother's home. Stacy Woods was a rather large man with flaming red hair. At the end of his teaching, he began to speak words of knowledge to those who were present. He looked at me and stated that he had a word from God. He said God had chosen us to go into full time service. And that thousands of people's lives would be affected.

I decided to seek counsel. I called the assistant pastor of our church, Jack Gustafson, to ask if we could get together. We agreed to meet for lunch at one of Medford's finest eating establishments. Over lunch I related to Jack all that had transpired over the past few months. His response was, "Dom, Gary and I and the rest of the staff have always felt that you should be in full time ministry. We have been waiting on the Lord to confirm it with you." I left our meeting with answers as to what God had in store for us. There were some personal issues that had to be resolved, and questions that needed divine intervention.

There were three main concerns that we needed clear direction from God. The main concern was the issue of divorce and remarriage. Second, was the age factor, going into the ministry in my early forties. Third, was I willing to give up a nice retirement package from the company and the earning potential that I had if I continued working for the corporation.

We placed all these matters in the hands of the Lord. Both Tricia and I like so many people today had been in a godless marriage, both ending in divorce. Our marriage started as a secular marriage, but when we were born again, the Lord transformed our lives into what I call a spiritual marriage, one founded in His principles and His love. We are "subject to one another in the fear of Christ" (Eph. 5:21).

After much prayer and seeking the will of God for our lives, God spoke to us through a dear brother in Christ, Jerry Lausmann, a Medford, Oregon businessman. Jerry was seeking the seat as the Congressman from the fourth Congressional District for Oregon. He asked if I would be interested in running his campaign as the campaign manager. Tricia and I prayed about it at length and decided that if God wanted us to be in full time ministry, this would be the way to force us out of the retail business.

We accepted the position through the primary elections. Jerry won the Republican primary with a landslide percentage, but due to some differences of campaign strategy, we decided to resign. We parted as good friends. This made it possible for us to move to San Mateo, California, where I matriculated at Simpson Bible College.

Prior to my conversion I was used to relying on my own abilities to meet our necessities, but I had to learn to trust in Him and His word. Always having plenty and being able to spend what I had earned, this was a great adjustment for both of us. Having to learn to be receivers rather than givers became a challenge to us. Having to change our philosophy about finances was a process that only a loving God could work out in our lives. We learned that God is faithful to His word, "And my God shall supply all your need according to His riches in glory by Christ Jesus" (Phil. 4:19).

The subject of divorce continued to haunt me and still bothers me to this day. While looking for a place to enroll in school we decided to visit some of our family in Southern California. We decided to attend Sunday services at The Church On the Way, in Van Nuys, California, having heard so much about the ministry of Pastor Jack Hayford. As Pastor Hayford was closing his message, he stopped and said he felt compelled by the Holy Spirit to speak to the hearts of those desiring and contemplating going into full time ministry, especially those who had gone through the anguish of divorce. I don't remember his exact words, but they were words of encouragement, that if God had called us, He would open doors for the work He had called us to. We left the services with great anticipation.

A few days later I called the offices of Church On the Way and spoke with Rev. Jack Hayford. He encouraged us to continue seeking God's will for our lives.

We visited Angeles Temple and spoke with the pastors, Dr. and Mrs. Howard Courtney, Sr. We were encouraged to pursue the call. When we seek Godly counsel from Elders in the body of Christ we will not fail. When we are truly born again, we are new creations.

I still feel the pain and pangs of going through a divorce. I remember the distrust I developed over some of the circumstances that led up to my divorce. These are scars that have since healed, but it took a commitment on my part to study the teachings of the Lord Jesus, who forgives and restores. Because Tricia and I have experienced divorce, we have been able to minister to hundreds of couples who are going through the pain and feelings of rejection. In most instances divorce is based on selfishness on the part of either or both, parties. It comes from a lack or willingness to live up to their marriage vows.

However what do we do with all those who have been divorced, those who are part of the body of Christ? Do we shun them from society, and exclude them from the body of Christ? No, we love and comfort them and teach them godly principles that will strengthen their marriages. They are not pariahs, but human beings made in the image of God. We are all sinners, yet saved by grace alone. We are to extend grace to all.

Chapter Four

Study To Show Yourself Approved

With a new perspective on ministry and what we believed was a direct leading from the Lord, we found ourselves moving to San Mateo, California. Tricia was able to find a job in Redwood City working for a paving & grading contractor. I started my tenure as a full time student at Simpson College, at that time located in San Francisco. One morning while eating breakfast the Lord clearly spoke to me about where we should fellowship.

We went to services at Kings Way Foursquare Church. I approached Pastor Randy Helton and asked him if I could make an appointment to see him the following week. I shared part of my testimony with him. I left nothing out as to my background, work ethics, my divorce and remarriage; that I was a full time student, but felt that the Lord had spoken clearly to me to submit to him as our new pastor. Whatever he wished me to do for the church, I was willing to do it, as my schedule allowed.

A week or so later, Randy approached me and asked me to come by and see him. I made an appointment with his secretary for the next week. Randy explained that he had spoken to the church council about us and that they had unanimously voted to offer me the position as assistant to Randy on a part time basis while I was enrolled at Simpson. I had been obedient to what God had spoken to my heart. God had opened doors for us to minister under Randy's tutelage.

Randy was able to procure a Western District license for me and later was instrumental in helping me attain International credentials. In 1987, in San Diego I received my ordination. We are in our 24th year of ministry and still have a deep passion to serve in whatever capacity the Lord wills.

Looking back at those early years of ministry and how the Lord guided our steps, I am amazed, as to how he takes people like Tricia and me, who have gone through so much emotional and physical pain and causes us to discover fruitful and fulfilling ministry in helping others.

Submit Unto God

While we were in San Mateo God used our tenure as assistant ministers to teach us certain Christian principles. One was in the area of submission.

For twenty years I had been in management, either middle or upper management. I was used to giving orders and expected people to carry them out. But in God's kingdom, He has called us to serve others. The Gospel of John describes our Lord as washing the disciple's feet: "For I have given you an example, that you should do as I have done to you" (John 13:15). God had to show me how to wash others' feet. This was a very difficult lesson to learn, since it dealt with my pride. It is a lesson that is repeated over and over.

Submission and servanthood go hand in hand. Paul the Apostle states, "And be subject to one another in the fear of Christ" (Eph.5:21). We are to learn to trust brothers and sisters in Christ. This is not blind obedience, but learning to love one another as God intends.

I was born during the Great Depression, an era that was extremely racist. Hispanics were treated as second class citizens. I had been scarred: by bigotry and racial slurs in my formative years. These emotional scars would surface later in life and cause grief and pain.

As a new Christian, I had to learn to look at all people of color and see them as Christ sees them. For years, I had to fight and work harder to be accepted and advance in the business world. Now I had to learn to trust God, and recognize that in His world there is no elite troupe: "For the Lord your God is God of gods and Lord of lords, the great God, mighty and awesome, who shows no partiality nor takes a bribe" (Dt. 10:17). When I fully grasped this Biblical concept, I was on the way to a needed healing in the area of discrimination. I'm not "naive" to think that race discrimination has been eradicated. But there have been great strides taken to right the wrongs that have permeated the Church at large.

I thank God for people like Randy and Tina Helton, who extended the hand of true Christian friendship and gave me opportunity. Under Randy's mentoring, we were being prepared for future ministry. When I graduated from Simpson Bible College I had a solid foundation in the Bible. Through Randy, I understood about church structure and dealing with some of the problems that arise in a healthy church.

In the fall of 1979 we met the Western District supervisor, Dr. Fred Wymore. With his blessing we started on a venture of visiting different communities in the northern part of California seeking God's will about pioneering a new Foursquare church.

In November 1979 we said goodbye to our friends in San Mateo and moved to Susanville, California.

In order for us to move to Susanville, I had to sell a Mexican $25.00 gold piece, worth about $480.00. With this and some money that I had received from a speaking engagement we started on our trek. For the next seven years we gave our lives to this beautiful little town nestled in the eastern side of the Sierras. It was a journey that would be a learning excursion, a path that impacted our lives in such a way that only a loving God can structure.

Chapter Five

Season Of Tent Making

I look back and realize how inept and unprepared we were for starting a church. We didn't have a clue as to how to begin. We had the promise of a couple to help us get started and we had made three or four ventures to the area. Both Tricia and I felt that we had a clear and direct leading from the Lord.

Through this couple we met another family who became the first members of this fledgling church. Gil and Kim had two young daughters, Janna and Leah, who made up our first Sunday school class. God had sent them to Susanville from an independent non-denominational church in Southern California, for the expressed purpose of helping start a pioneer work in this area. It never ceases to amaze me the way God guides each step of our lives when it pertains to spreading the gospel.

As I stated above, we were totally unprepared for what awaited us in birthing a church. We were to spend the next seven years investing our lives in souls that the Lord placed in our care to nurture. These years were to be years of learning.

I have always been self-motivated, needing very little guidance. I sometimes think God must chuckle at the circumstances I get myself into, but He has always been at my side. His patience has taught me not to be so self-reliant.

God opened a door of ministry in the form of a weekly radio program that was aired on Sunday mornings. We started the program a few weeks after we arrived and did the broadcast until our departure seven years later. I approached the local secular radio station owner/manager shortly after our arrival. And asked him if he had any open times for a Christian broadcast. He stated that at the present time all the time slots were filled. He went on to explain that since his was the only station in the area, he rarely had any openings. I left with what I felt was an empty promise. If radio time became available, he would consider us. And placed us on the waiting list.

I left with a void in my heart, but God was at work without my help. A few weeks passed and I received a call from the station owner who expressed he didn't know why, but he felt led to give me a half- hour time slot over others who were waiting for an opening on the list. Our program was not live, but taped weekly to be played on Sunday mornings at 10 A.M. At times, people would stop me on the street and say they had heard me on Sunday morning. Some stated they had asked Christ into their hearts.

Radio ministry can't be measured by secular standards, for only God knows how many people are either saved or taught biblical principles. People who listen to radio ministry are often going through a difficult time in their marriage due to a divorce, the loss of a loved one, or the death of a spouse, people with feelings of despair and loneliness. Some feel deserted by humanity. Some are mad at God for their circumstances in life. Others are disenchanted with organized religion. Many of these people are unsaved and completely out of tune as to the function of the body of Christ.

Today I see more clearly why God had us on radio. We were planting seeds of comfort and compassion to hurting people who would find it difficult to fellowship in an organized setting. Because of the learning experience of the small radio medium in our early years in the pastorate, unknown to us God would allow us to have another radio ministry outreach where we currently serve.

Our First Gathering Place

When we moved to Susanville we didn't have a place to meet. It had never entered our minds that we might run into problems in renting or leasing a suitable facility. The first week we were there we went to the Chamber of Commerce to see if they knew of any vacant buildings. To their knowledge there was none available. They directed us to the Catholic Church hall located directly across from the chamber building. As we entered the hall we met a man whose name was Paul. Paul was in charge of renting and maintaining the building. I explained that we had been led by the Lord to start a fellowship in this town and that we were from the Foursquare denomination. He stated to me that he was a Charismatic Catholic filled with the Holy Spirit, and believed that the gifts were for today. He rented us the hall and we conducted our first service on December 2, 1979.

Paul and his wife became close friends, but never became regulars in our church. They attended on special occasions. I was greatly honored when I was asked to officiate as Paul and Diane renewed their marriage vows.

Again we saw the Lord's hand in our lives. He was birthing His church and He was using a willing vessel. At times, we place far too much emphasis on our church denominations, polity, and structure. We leave out the most important ingredient, the work of the Holy Spirit. The book of Act's states it so succinctly by saying, "Set apart for Me Barnabas and Saul for the work to which I have called them" (Acts 13:2). God the Holy Spirit used Paul to be a "Barnabas" to Tricia and me. Paul and Diane and their family later moved to Hawaii.

I would like to emphasize a very important principle. It is my belief that God has to train and prepare us for ministry on a continual basis. Bible College and seminary teach us theology, ministry skills, philosophy, and how to study the Word of God. What college and seminary fails to teach is how to minister to people. God's lessons are the life experiences He allows us to experience. The four Gospels clearly show the care that Jesus took in preparing His disciples for future ministry. In the early years of our ministry God was preparing Tricia and me for our present ministry. Even before I was a believer, God was working in my life although I was unaware of His presence.

In 1958 I was working for a large retail corporation as a management trainee. A co-worker had recently been appointed as the new assistant manager of the store. I myself was at home recuperating from surgery when I was informed that this man had been hospitalized for exploratory surgery.

Unbeknown to me his family had requested no visitors. I went to see him and took a small gift to cheer him up. When I got to his room his face lit up and you could see by his smile that he was glad to see me. He asked how I was recuperating from my recent surgery. I remember thanking him for his concern. He stated to me that he hoped to see me at work again in the near future.

This was the last time I was to see him alive. He was sent home to die a few days later. When they operated on him they discovered that cancer had spread throughout his body. Here was a man 38-years-old with a wife and two children, destined to die a few months later. Forty years later, I still feel sadness in my heart for him and his family. What I was feeling at the time was compassion.

God prepares us throughout all our lives to serve Him. Sometimes we are oblivious to His workings. Jesus stated, "And when did we see You sick, or in prison and come to You? And the King will answer and say to them, Truly I say to you, to the extent that you did it to one of these brothers of mine, even the least of them, you did it to Me" Matt. (25:39-40). At that time, though I was an agnostic, God's hand was on my life. God used me to minister to this man who was dying a horrible death though I had no clue as to what being a Christian was all about.

Prison Ministry

A state penitentiary is located approximately eight miles outside Susanville. In 1980 there were only 12 prisons in the state of California. The inmate population in the state was around 38,000; today, the inmate population has grown to over 140,000. The prison population in Susanville at that time was around 1,000 inmates.

I was invited by the Protestant Chaplain to tour the facility and to conduct weekly Bible studies. I remember how I felt as I walked through the double security doors and wondered how the inmates must feel. Once they close the doors behind you; you cannot retrace your steps.

In addition I was to discover how those who are incarcerated deal with their emotions and how they interact in a hostile environment.

The chaplain had been afflicted with the advance stages of amyothropic lateral sclerosis, known as Lou Gherig's disease. He could barely communicate and was totally reliant on a prisoner to provide for his basic needs. The inmate had to lift the man into a

29

wheel chair each day and help him with all his personal functions. His theology was extremely liberal in nature. I felt pity for the man and sorrow for his bitterness. He had been married and divorced and never gotten over the rejection from his daughter and his ex-wife.

A few months after I started helping him at the institution his condition deteriorated to the point where he was unable to continue. One of the most haunting sights that I have ever seen was when they wheeled him out of the prison to a waiting car, not able to lift his head. Later he succumbed to this ravaging disease. What is still an enigma to me is that he never preached Christ to the inmates. I am still saddened by all the lives he failed to touch.

One of life's lessons that the Lord allowed me to experience was in the area of compassion. When we are compassionate to others we are being as Christ would have us be. I've often contemplated whether or not my chaplain friend ever had a change of heart and asked Jesus into his heart prior to his death.

I was asked by one of the prison officials if I would be interested in being the full time Chaplain? After spending time in prayer and discussion with my wife, I felt obligated to decline the offer. The Lord had called us to the area to start a church, and not be distracted with a full time commitment to a chaplaincy in a controlled environment. I expressed, however, that I would act as an interim Chaplain until they were able to hire a replacement. I was to act in this capacity for several months.

The prison system is very complex as to the incarceration of inmates. The State of California penal infrastructure rates or numbers the prisoners according to the severity of their crimes and the amount of times they have been incarcerated prior to their current offense. Thus they are rated either level one, two, three or four. Level three and four inmates are hard core criminals. The nature of the crime and one's prior convictions determines in most cases where they will be confined. The Susanville Correctional facility at that time was a level one and two.

There is a self-imposed code maintained by the inmates that can be extremely difficult for a new prisoner and is, at times, life threatening. I would describe it as a pecking order. If you are an inmate you are expected to live by the convict rule. You don't snitch, because if you do, chances are they will kill you or inflict such strong physical punishment that you may wish you were dead. If you survive the attack you will do most of your time in protective custody.

Another unwritten code is the group with which you choose to be associated. In California state prisons the convict population is approximately 41% black and 42% Latino. Within these two dominant ethnic groups there are rival gangs. In the black prison community there are the Crypts and Bloods: in the Latino population you have the Latino gangs, Nortenios (Northern) and Surenios (Southern). There is a constant battle for dominance. They self-segregate themselves. Blacks eat among themselves and the Latinos eat-within their respective groups. There is a constant daily friction. The pressure placed on a new inmate to choose their clique can create a tremendous amount of emotional strain.

One of the most tragic incidents occurred at the institution shortly after I started ministering to the inmates. A young Latino from the state of Texas came to me with a problem. He was being harassed maliciously and being threatened with his life if he failed to chose which group he would side with. His only desire was to complete his time and go home to Texas. He had almost four years to serve on his sentence and was asking about being placed in protective custody. A few days later, while in the prison yard, he was attacked by other convicts and was taken to the infirmary. I later learned that the other inmates had taken both of his hands and broken them in the wringer of a mop-bucket.

Prison life is violent. The daily emotional strain placed on inmates is immeasurable. The young man recovered and was placed in protective custody in order to spare his life.

Another young man had been convicted of rape. For some reason, he was placed in solitary confinement. He was watched by the guards around the clock, and was given only the bare necessities of life. He lived in a cell without TV or any of the privileges given to other inmates. I was asked by one of the prison guards to visit him. This was the first time I had visited the hole. I was entranced by the sterility of the unit. I was reminded of the Apostle Paul and Silas being incarcerated in Phillippi and how they ministered to the jailer and other prisoners (Acts 16). They shared the good news of the Gospel and souls were won for Christ.

This young man had asked to see me because of his emotional state of mind. He was suffering from depression and other mental issues that he needed to resolve. He had gotten into a fight with another inmate and had resisted the guards. He was only 20 years old. He was tall, and large-framed. We exchanged greetings, talked for a few minutes and then I prayed with him.

A few days later they found him dead in his cell. He had taken his own life by hanging. As I look back at this tragedy could it have been avoided? His life had been one of destruction and he died violently. He confessed that he was a Christian and attended chapel services and Bible Studies on a regular basis, but his mind was so twisted and warped that he was unable to cope with the prison environment.

There are thousands just like him. They are seldom healed from the mental abuse they have to live with on a daily basis. Scripture teaches us to "Remember the prisoners, as though in prison with them, and those who are ill-treated, since you yourselves are in the body" (Heb. 13:3). We are to remember them in prayer and visit them when feasible. God can then touch their hearts and they, in turn, can give their lives over to Christ.

We must recognize the reality that these men and women are incarcerated for crimes committed against society. In most cases they have reaped what they have sown. On the other hand they are God's creation and deserve to be treated as such. We are to love them while hating the crimes they have perpetrated. The men and women who have chosen to work in this hostile environment also need our prayers. Each day they are placed in dangerous situations.

While we were in Susanville, Tricia and I developed a good rapport with most of the officers. In fact, many became members of our church. Some were instructors who taught various classes to the inmates and many of them are still members of the Susanville Foursquare Church.

The prison culture over the last 20 years has changed dramatically. When I started at the Susanville correctional facility the inmate population was close to a thousand men; today it has swelled to close to 11,000 men. The state has constructed another facility that is a level three and four institution. They have also had to increase the number of camps where they place the men who fight fires during the fire season. These are inmates who are serving short sentences and need less supervision.

There are currently 33 state prisons in the state of California, with over 140,000 thousand inmates. As a society we have failed to curb the tide of violence. As Christians we can make an impact if we develop outreach ministries to the young before they seek a life of violence and crime.

According to a recent report, nation wide crime had decreased. It is reportedly the lowest it has been in many years. Yet we continue to construct larger, more sophisticated institutions to house the perpetrators, based on the nature of their offenses.

The age of the inmate population has decreased. There are younger and more violent offenders. For the most part, prisons do not rehabilitate men and women; instead they educate the inmates to a higher level of criminality so that they are more vicious and violent.

In my current position as Chaplain in Salinas, I work very close with the officers who transport and guard inmates who are hospitalized. They express how the nature of the convicts has changed. Since inmates are younger and more violent, they have become more confrontational and highly aggressive. Most have gang affiliations on the outside and work in tandem against the guards while in prison. Since the inmates belong to a gang they consider themselves part of a large family within the prison system. This in turn places the officers at greater risk.

Assaults on correctional officers are at an all time high. Violence has escalated drastically in the prisons. We are educating young men and women to a more cold and calculating behavior because when they are released into society they will commit more heinous and felonious crimes.

The United States has a horrific youth gang problem that has reached pandemic proportions. Our state and youth institutions are swelling to overflowing due to a moral crisis in our society. The escalation of divorce and the rise of illegitimacy have created a subclass of humanity. Many of the young men and women who are initiated into gangs are third and fourth generation gang members. Most gang members consider the gang as their family. How do you separate yourself from your family?

Another component prevalent with all gang members is that they dare not show fear. Fear is a sign of weakness and if you are going to be part of a gang, or are incarcerated, fear is the one emotion that you cannot express.

Moses speaking to the Israelite's before entering Canaan warned them about keeping the law. "Assemble the people, the men and women and children and the alien who is in your town, in order that they may hear and learn to fear the Lord your God, and be careful to observe all the words of this law. And their children, who have not known, will hear and learn to fear the Lord your God, as long as your live on the land which you are about to cross the Jordan to possess" (Deut. 31:12-13). Fear comes from knowing that there is a God.

There is a generation of young people who do not fear God because they do not know Him. If our nation is going to see a decline in gangs and crimes they commit, then the church needs to be more assertive in its outreach to young people of all racial backgrounds. We need to pray that God will bind the "strong man." We are dealing with a supernatural, spiritual problem. Jesus said, "Or how can anyone enter the strong man's house and carry off his property, unless he first binds the strong man?" (Matt, 12:29a).

The gang problem in the United States will not resolve itself, or be eradicated, until we as a society become convinced that there is a social crisis among our youth. Christians must take the initiative by going back into the inner cities and re-establishing ministries and healthy churches there. Inner city people feel that the church has deserted them. And there is some truth in what they say. The church can make a difference if it is willing to evangelize the lost. It must obey the great commission. "Go into all the world and preach the gospel to every creature" (Mk.16:15).

Chapter Six

Laying Hand's On The Sick

I became very active in the local ministerial association made up of representatives of different Protestant denominations. The association operated a very active food bank and an on-call hospital chaplain's ministry. During Easter week there were ecumenical services generally on Good Friday.

The hospital ministry was a rotating on-call service. The chaplain was given a beeper for a week and was on-call Sunday through Saturday. Because the hospital was a very small facility; major surgery or acute care patients had to be transported to Reno, Nevada or air lifted to Redding, California.

I will never forget my first funeral as a minister in Susanville. While I was on call as chaplain for the first time I received an emergency call from the hospital. When I arrived at the hospital I was greeted by a pediatric specialist from Reno, who periodically held clinics in Susanville; he ushered me into a surgical room. On the examining table was the body of a small infant. Much to my horror the baby had bruises all over her body as well as a broken arm. Her little arm was in a splint, or cast, as I was best able to determine. The physician surmised that the baby had been abused and I was asked to speak with the parents concerning the demise of the child. I met with the parents who seemed very distraught. I tried to be compassionate even though they were under suspicion for abusing the child and her ultimate death.

The parents told me that a baby sitter had abused the child while the mother was visiting her family back east for a few weeks. The mother claimed that the baby had been fine until she returned home to the Susanville area. They asked if I would officiate at the child's funeral. I agreed to do the graveside services.

I felt numb as I prepared for the funeral. Bible College had not prepared me for the type of emotions I was feeling. I did not want to be judgmental regarding the guilt or innocence of the parents. I felt that if they were guilty of causing the death of this baby, then the civil authorities would have to judge them. I was called a few weeks later by the local police department to give a deposition. There were no arrest made in the case. The couple came to church a few times, but there was something amiss in their relationship. I later found out they had lost their first child, not to death, but the state had placed the child in protective custody for abuse.

Life brings many heartaches and emotional traumas. Pain and suffering are felt in more ways than just physical. Emotional pain is the most difficult to deal with. Over the course of my five years as a full time chaplain I have seen the pain and suffering that people feel at the loss of a baby or when babies are born with defects that will cause them to die at an early age.I can look back at Susanville in retrospect and see God's plan unfold in my current ministry. I am amazed at the manner God works. He is the one who brings comfort and wisdom. He teaches regarding life and death. He differentiates what is superficial and what is supernatural. He desires to heal feelings and relationships.

One day as I was making rounds, I noticed a woman who I surmised was in her middle fifties, sitting in a chair next to a window. She looked extremely depressed and was about to burst out crying. In the bed next to her was a younger woman whose face was grotesquely disfigured. She had the advanced stages of cancer of the facial glands. When I introduced myself to the older woman and told her that I was a minister her demeanor changed. She informed me that she was the patient's mother and that her daughter could pass away at any time. Her daughter was in a coma and would slip in and out of coherency. I asked if I could pray. Without hesitation she responded, "Please." I prayed that the Lord would give her strength and peace regarding the coming demise of her daughter. The words she spoke were words of despair, a pleading of the heart that yearned for comfort. I heard a mother's anguish for her daughter who was suffering pain.

After I prayed for the mother, I asked if she would permit me to anoint her daughter with oil and pray for her. I prayed that Christ would bring peace and healing to her ravaged body and perform a miracle.

36

By this time there was a different look on the mother's face. Jesus had brought her peace. She was able to accept the fact that her daughter was dying and that her daughter's soul and spirit were in His care. I told her I would come back the next day.

I returned to the hospital the next day and proceeded to the dying woman's room. As I entered the room I noticed that she was awake propped up on pillows. A smile was on her disfigured face as she raised a feeble hand and waved. I could hardly contain myself. The mother greeted me with a smile and again thanked me for coming. The cancer had eaten so much of the daughter's face and throat that she was unable to speak. But the look in her eyes said so much. They were eyes that said; "Thank you, God bless you for your concern and compassion." A few days later, the young woman died and was interred in the local cemetery. Later I read the obituaries about her age and how many children she and her husband had. I thought about the void that was left in this family by the passing of a young wife and mother.

Jesus promised, "Peace I leave with you; My peace I give to you, not as the world gives, do I give to you. Let not your heart be troubled, nor let it be fearful" (John 14:27). He brought peace to a dying woman and her mother. I was to be the vessel that brought comfort in time of need to a mother who felt helpless and was about to lose her daughter.

Jesus also said, "Truly, truly, I say to you, he who believes in Me, the works that I do shall he do also; and greater works than these shall he do; because I go to the Father" (John 14:12). Christ is our example and the Holy Spirit is our guide.

I never asked if they were believers or if they attended church on a regular basis. I ministered with one thought in mind, "How would Jesus have dealt with these women?" We must never loose sight of the fact that we are His creation and, as such, we represent Jesus as His ambassadors.

Full of Grace and Truth

It was 1:30 AM. The phone rang wakening me out of a sound sleep. It was the extended care facility at the local hospital. The nurse on duty asked if I could come right away to the unit. One of the elderly patients was about to expire. She had requested to see a pastor or priest. I dressed and rushed to the hospital and was immediately taken to a small sterile room. I was told that the woman had no close relatives living in or close to Susanville. There was a nephew who lived out of state and they would notify him in the morning.

As I approached her bed the elderly woman responded. I asked if she was ready to meet the Lord? She related to me that she had not been very religious. As a child she had been baptized a Roman Catholic, but had never kept her vows. Through the years she had tried other religions, but never seemed to follow through. She asked me if I would hear her confession and bless her. I explained that Jesus loved her and that if she asked Him to forgive her He would do so. It was extremely difficult for her to speak; she would drift off and then awaken. She tried to make the sign of the cross. I started to pray for her and told her that Jesus forgave her for the sins she had committed. She fell asleep and later in the night expired.

God the creator cares for His creation. I am forever grateful and thankful to Him for using me to bring comfort to this precious woman. Because God is faithful and true to His word, He honored her request and He forgave her. The book of Romans states, "If you confess with your mouth Jesus as Lord and believe in your heart that God raised Him from the dead, you shall be saved; for with the heart man believes, resulting in righteousness, and with the mouth he confesses, resulting in salvation" (Rom.10:9-10).

Here was a lonely dying woman who during her entire adult life had neglected to honor Jesus. She died a lonely broken woman without friends or relatives at her side, but she died knowing that Jesus would welcome her into His kingdom. What Grace!

Over the years this same scenario has been repeated many times. The woman whom I ministered to that night was a seed that God planted in my heart to help me minister to the elderly. There were to be many more incidents of tragedy and sorrow, some more painful than others. Many had good endings while others were heart wrenching, but Gods plan and desire is for all to come to know Him through His son, Christ the Savior. We saw God's plan unfold in our lives daily as we sought His guidance by prayer and a commitment to His word. "The steps of a man are established by the Lord; and He delights in his way" (Psalm 37:23). God was guiding each step of our lives and He was delighted in our ways. We chose to follow and serve, and He directed our paths. We made many mistakes, but God used them to sharpen and hone our skills.

Physician Heal Thyself

The year prior to our leaving Susanville a young boy died. His death was to impact or lives dramatically. Those who had direct contact with him were men and women in the medical profession. My wife and I were especially close to the situation because for a short time I had been his pastor. The doctors who were attending to the boy's physical needs were very strong in their Christian beliefs. Because of the way they conducted themselves I gained a greater respect for them and the entire medical profession.

I received a call asking me to report to the hospital for an emergency concerning one of my parishioners. When Tricia and I arrived at the hospital the parents of the boy were waiting for us. Since the parents no longer attended our church I wondered why they had contacted me.

My thoughts raced back to when I had first met this couple. Their Christian doctrine was distorted. Our first conversation was concerning spousal separation and divorce. Part of our discussion focused on alcoholism. The husband was a recovering alcoholic and was having difficulty in his commitment to Christ and the 12-step program.

Theologically we were miles apart when it came to the issue of divorce and remarriage and other doctrinal issues. The woman was a self-appointed "prophetess." She felt that if a wife was more spiritually mature than her husband she was "unequally yoked" and, therefore, she could divorce her husband. She had been married five times and I later heard that she eventually left her current husband, the father of the boy. She had assumed the role, as spiritual leader of the family and continually usurped the authority of her husband. The woman had started Bible studies in her home for women only. She was able to confuse several women and this led them to divorce their husbands devastating entire families. Interestingly, she called me in her hour of need.

My thoughts brought me back to the crisis at hand. I was told that the doctors were in the boy's room attending him and that his condition was extremely critical. After praying and asking God for comfort, I reassured the family that the boy was in the Lord's hands.

A nurse came and stated that the physicians wanted me to come into the room where the youth was and pray for him. I remember seeing the child with all the hospital paraphernalia attached to his body. I had known the 12 year-old youth when he was full of life, but now he was in a coma fighting for his life. They had placed him in a special bed to keep his body temperature down. As I approached the bed I looked around the room and noticed the look of despair, frustration, and apprehension in some and total lassitude in the face of all. As I entered the room the faces changed to one of hope. Was it because I was minister? Or because my prayers were being answered in that instant, prayers that God would bring peace to the situation. The boy was to be airlifted to Washaw Medical Facility in Reno, Nevada.

The primary physician was a man whom I respect and admire as a physician and as a brother in Christ. He was my personal physician for all the years that I resided in Susanville. He invited me to lead this small group of concerned health care givers in prayer. Asking that God's hand be on the entire situation, I again prayed for divine peace to reign over this crisis.

After I finished praying, the doctor fell on my neck and wept like a baby. His tears were tears of sorrow and grief. Everyone in the room was weeping, including myself. Our common grief seemed to somehow lift the heaviness from our shoulders.

Thoughts raced through my mind regarding these circumstances and why everyone was crying. I pondered how cold the boy's body felt, as if his spirit had already departed. The doctors who had taken an oath to strive to prolong and protect life felt helpless and ineffective as they wept over there inability to save the boy's life. They were facing the fact that it is God Himself who has power over life and death.

To this day I have treasured that moment when I saw men and women draw closer to God and each other because of the circumstances they were involved in. God used me to bring comfort to others in that particular place and time. We all reach a point when only God can bring peace.

Later that night I helped place the boy into the helicopter for the flight to Reno where he was taken to Washaw Medical Center and placed in the Intensive Care unit. He was scheduled for exploratory surgery the next day, but unfortunately, he succumbed shortly after he arrived in Reno.

His death because of his youth, seemed tragic, but Isaiah the prophet wrote "The righteous man perishes, and no man takes it to heart; and devout men are taken away, while no one understands, for the righteous man is taken away from evil" (Isa. 57:1). I feel that God spared this young boy from a life filled with evil.

An autopsy was done on the boy after his death. They found a cyst at the base of his spine that placed pressure on his brain. In turn, the pressure formed fluid on the brain, which later caused his death.

Later the mother sued the doctors for malpractice. I was never called to testify and do not know if a judgement was given to the parents, but my heart wants to believe that the courts found in favor of the doctors.

Could his death have been avoided? Could medical science have saved him? Was the medical attention he received the best care possible? I cannot answer these questions but I did learn something from this experience. I would agree with Paul the Apostle who wrote in his letter to the church at Corinth, "Even so the thoughts of God no one knows except the Spirit of God" (I Cor. 2:11b). I believe that it was God who allowed this young boy to live a few short years and it was God who took him home.

As a minister and Chaplain I sense God's presence while praying for people. God gives strength to the afflicted. His word states: "Blessed be the God and Father of our Lord Jesus Christ, the Father of mercies and God of all comfort; who comforts us in all our affliction. So that we may be able to comfort those who are in any affliction with the comfort with which we ourselves are comforted by God" (II Cor. 1:3-4).

It is ironic that the ones who needed God's comfort most seemed to be the health care workers. I never saw the boy's parents again, but through this incident I developed a closer relationship with the physicians and nurses at our community hospital. I still feel pain and sorrow for the mother who was so easily misled. Though God is a forgiving and loving God and loves her as He loved her son, She has to live with the choices that she made.

Chapter Seven

Rule Over The Animals

One night around 12:30 am I received a phone call from a man who asked if I would please come to his home. He sounded intoxicated and I was concerned that he might take his own life. I wrote the directions hurriedly on a piece of paper and went into the cold night. He lived at the end of a lonely country road. The home was located close to where the local deer migrate to fill themselves on the local alfalfa fields.

You probably know if you live in mountain country, that it is extremely dangerous to drive at night on country roads, because of the habits of deer. They graze at night and will cross country roads at will. Where I was headed was one of the most densely populated deer habitats in California.

As I approached the man's driveway I asked the Lord to give me peace and wisdom. I was not prepared for what awaited me. I knocked on the door and a voice invited me in. I opened the door and, to my surprise, I was greeted by hundreds of cats. My eyes scanned the living room and came to rest on a man sitting in a large armchair surrounded by felines of every color, size and shape.

He introduced himself to me and proceeded to tell me why he had called. The man was in his middle sixties. As I had suspected, he was inebriated. He was not dressed for the cold mountain weather since it was in the dead of winter. His garb consisted of a pair of blue jeans and underwear. The years of heavy drinking had taken its toll on him physically. He had a ponderous stomach and a huge scar on his abdomen, evidence of his first attempt at suicide.

He proceeded to relate to me the pathetic and chaotic life he had lived. He had struggled with alcoholism all of his adult life. Several times he had decided to take his life, but each time had either failed or changed his mind. The lamentable fact was that he had attended a Bible college and had studied for the ministry.

My heart went out to this man and I felt saddened at how unfruitful his life had been. I was reminded of the parable of the talents, "And to one he gave five talents, to another, two, and to another, one, each according to his own ability" (Matt. 25:15). As I listened it was obvious to me that he was intelligent and had once had a relationship with Christ, a relationship that became tarnished by his wasting the talent he had been given. He was full of guilt and felt that God would not forgive him of his sins. I assured him of God's availability.

As I prayed for this man I brought some comfort to him. He had listened to me on the radio and felt I could help him. I told him I would be available to talk with him anytime, and that he was welcome to come to fellowship at our church.

I met him on several occasions in town at restaurants, but he never came to church. At various times when he was drunk, he would telephone me, but he never called again regarding ending his life. He later died of a massive heart attack.

Could I have done more for this man? The answer is "no" for only God can deliver from addiction. Moreover the individual must deal with the problem himself. This man needed deliverance from other issues that he refused to face. He could have used professional help for his drug and alcohol addiction. He had spent his entire life feeling sorry for himself rather than confronting the real problem. He was hoping God would send instant deliverance. He didn't want to pay the price of self-discipline.

Jesus dealt with people's motivations on numerous occasions. Consider the man at the pool of Bethesda. The Bible says, "And a certain man was there, who had been thirty-eight years in his sickness. When Jesus saw him lying there, and knew that he had already been a long time in that condition, He said to him, 'Do you wish to get well?' The sick man answered him, 'Sir, I have no man to put me into the pool when the water is stirred up, but while I am coming, another steps down before me.' Jesus said to him, 'Arise, take up your pallet, and walk" (John 5:5-8).

The man got up and walked. Jesus later found him in the temple and told him not to sin anymore so that nothing worse would happen to him (John 5:14). Jesus recognized that the man's condition was due to a condition of his heart, blatant sin. Alcoholism is a sin and we must treat it as such; yet we must have compassion for those who are addicted.

A certain segment of society believes that people with certain types of addiction are victims. Therefore, if we are victims, we do not bare responsibility for our actions. When we start recognizing sin for what it is we will see God bring deliverance.

Alcohol abuse can and will destroy lives. As a boy, I saw the ravages of alcohol on members of my own family. There were relatives on both sides of my parent's families who were addicted to alcohol. I remember my father's brother going through withdrawals, delirium tremors (DTs). He was going through self-detoxification.

Though some go through detoxification on their own, others check themselves into a medical facility where drugs help them go through the recovery process with out so much trauma. I can still remember my uncle's screams about snakes and spiders crawling over him. I was five years old at the time and it is still vivid in my mind to this day.

The United States is the number one consumer of alcohol in the world. Teen alcoholism is at an all time high and is on the rise. Drug addiction among youth continues to soar. The Bible mentions "visiting the inequity of the fathers on the children, on the third and fourth generation of those who hate Me" (Ex. 20:5). Almost everything humans do is a learned behavior. Many are taught to drink by their parents. If we truly love God we will teach our children to abstain from using alcohol.

Unless the Church takes a more active role in winning souls for Christ we will see a generation of young people lost for eternity. God, our heavenly Father, is merciful and compassionate, but unless we declare that He is also a God who judges sin, and that there is a literal hell for those who deny Him, many souls will be lost.

If Jesus can heal the sick and raise the dead, can He not also deliver those from the bondage of alcohol and drug addiction? Yes!

Living Water

Early in my ministry the Holy Spirit taught me a principle that I had failed to grasp as a young Christian. While I was preparing a sermon God revealed to me that I lacked a particular gift of the Spirit in ministering to His sheep.

A sermon should challenge people to a stronger commitment to God and encourage them to live a life of holiness. I was preparing such a sermon when something was triggered in my subconscious mind. When I first went into the ministry I had a preconceived concept about how a sermon was to touch lives. My homiletics however lacked one important ingredient-love.

I was preparing a study on Paul's teaching to the saints at Corinth the proper usage of spiritual gifts. As I was reading the Holy Spirit spoke to my spirit concerning Paul's words, "But earnestly desire the greater gifts. And I show you a still more excellent way" (I Cor. 12:31). The next chapter deals with this "more excellent way" love in action. The Holy Spirit then guided me to Romans 5:5. "And hope does not disappoint, because the love of God has been poured out within our hearts through the Holy Spirit who was given to us," God's love is a supernatural gift. So each time I minister, I am to reflect that pure love, so pure, a love that is giving and caring, rather than self- seeking. God gives the believer His love to use in His name.

In John 4 we read about the woman at the well who, by Jewish standards, was considered an outcast and harlot by her own people. She had been married five times and was now living with a man. She was half Jew and half Gentile, a Samaritan and the Jewish people had nothing to do with the Samaritans. The Savior of the world, though tired from His journey, had a dialogue with this wanton sinner.

This story depicts what Christianity is about. Jesus gave us an example to follow in trying to reach the lost. He came to save the lost and bring hope to the world. Rather than judge, we are to extend grace and share the truth in love.

Jesus extended an invitation for her to repent. He loved this woman because she was one of His lambs, one of His flock. His love touched her need.

Because Jesus loves me, He forgives me. When I have not lived up to the standard He set, my heart is pained. God's love for the believer is constant and as it flows to us it grows as we use it. It is the living water that flows from Christ.

This passage of scripture changed my entire approach in ministering to people. We are to extend grace and truth to all, regardless of their life styles. Grace is the living water. Jesus met a need in a sinner; we are to do the same.

My Peace I Give to You

There is not a human alive that does not at times struggle with their emotions, especially fear. I do not believe that Jesus anticipated a perfect world when He stated, "Peace I leave with you; My peace I give to you; not as the world gives, do I give to you. Let not your heart be troubled, nor let it be fearful" (John 14:27). This promise has become one of great inspiration and guidance. His peace is a gift in times of stress, pressure, anxiety and fears.

Our church family in Susanville had its normal challenges-family breakups, children being born out of wedlock, divorce and remarriage, infidelity, and even child molestation and incest. God ruled supreme in these challenges. Our lives were full and blessed. The experiences were challenging and we learned much about ministry.

The radio ministry was very rewarding and effective in touching lives in ways we could not measure. Our prison outreach was a ministry where we saw hundreds of men's lives impacted. Tricia and I treasure these years deeply and still miss the fellowship we had with the men behind prison walls.

During this time I developed a urinary condition that was later diagnosed as a chronic prostate inflammation. It was extremely painful. My physician prescribed antibiotics and the condition seemed to improve. A few days after I stopped taking the prescribed medication the symptoms recurred. After further tests the doctor suggested that x-rays be taken.

After reviewing the x-rays, the doctor asked Tricia and me to come to his office right away. We arrived at his office, concerned that he may have found cancer. He started to explain to me the options and treatment for bone cancer. I was almost numb with shock when he showed me the x-ray of my pelvic region.

He asked me if I had any type of insurance. My reply was no, but I told him that because I was a Korean Army Veteran I qualified for medical assistance at any Veteran's hospital. He stated that he was a good friend of the hospital administrator in the VA hospital in Reno and he would call him and have me admitted right away. As we left his office we had mixed feelings. In his office we had prayed that God would intervene and that His peace would reign in this ordeal.

We arrived at the Veterans hospital in Reno late that same evening. They admitted me to the Cancer ward, where I was treated with kindness and dignity. One of the nurses who cared for me was so gentle. She expressed great compassion that only Christ could give. While the doctors ordered various tests, I experienced a peace that I had never felt in my Christian walk. One test having to do with nuclear medicine. The patient is given an injection into their veins of a radiation active substance that is traced by a machine that x-rays your entire body. It took nearly two hours and I had to lie perfectly still while the machine passed over the entire length of my body. My thoughts wandered back and forth over events in my life. I was still able to thank God in this very trying time. The peace that our Lord spoke of in the Gospel of John sustained me.

The tests were later diagnosed as arthritis in the hip joints. The first diagnosis had been incorrect, but God allowed me to go through this ordeal in order to prepare us for further ministry to the sick.

The prostate problem became a chronic condition and over the next eight years continued to resurface.

Shortly after we moved to Salinas they detected the early stages of cancer of the prostate. On the 28th of June 1993, I was operated on for a radical Prostatectomy. Thank the Lord for the specialist who performed the procedure and the method he used for early detection.

One of the problems with men in ministry is pride. Most pastors feel it is a sign of weakness or a lack of faith should they get sick. In reality, however, many men and women leave the ministry because they have a hard time coping with personal illness.

The ordeal concerning cancer changed my life in a positive way. God did not inflict me with cancer of the prostate gland. He allowed me to experience the emotion's people with cancer experience, so that when I encounter a person who is suffering the emotional or physical pain of a carcinoma, I can identify with their needs.

When I needed peace in my life God was true to His word. His peace engulfed me. The prayers offered daily on my behalf also strengthened me. He heard our prayers for peace and as always gave us peace beyond all comprehension.

There are numerous scriptures that gave me strength and hope, but one that has been meaningful to me during some of the trials that I have encountered is, "I will never desert you, nor will I ever forsake you" (Heb. 13:5c). Christ, through the Holy Spirit, comforts us in times of need. We are the sheep of His pasture and are sustained by Him in times of trial and stress. He is always there for us.

In times of crisis we often forget that God is with us. We are not alone in our moments of despair. James writes "consider it all joy my brethren, when you encounter various trials, knowing that the testing of your faith produces endurance. And let endurance have its perfect result, that you may be perfect and complete, lacking nothing" (James 1:3-5). God allows us to experience all sorts of trials and tribulations to test our faith. The testing produces an inner strength that sees us through the trial. I call this faith in action.

Peter wrote, "In this you greatly rejoice, even though now for a little while, if necessary, you have been distressed by various trials" (I Peter 1:6). We will always have trials that will be full of stress, pain and sorrow, but the rewards are worth it.

"Be anxious for nothing, but in everything by prayer and supplication with thanksgiving let your request be made known to God. And the peace of God, which surpasses all comprehension, shall guard your hearts and your minds in Christ Jesus" (Phil. 4:6-7). Just imagine that our minds and hearts are being guarded by God's peace! God's peace is not a feeling; it is a supernatural act of an Omnipotent God who loves us. If you are going through a difficult time in your life, why not ask our Lord to intervene on your behalf? Ask Him for His peace. He will give it to you, "for the gifts and calling of God are irrevocable" (Rom. 11:29). He gives without measure.

In diagnosing of an illness it is always important to get a second opinion. You can prevent a lot of grief and anxious moments by not over reacting to the first diagnosis. Most doctors are well qualified in their specialty. But in my experience as a hospital chaplain and a pastor, I have learned that we are human and as such are prone to error in all phases of our respective professions. Doctors can make mistakes in their diagnosis. Have confidence in your physician as to his specialty. Most of the physicians that I know personally will send you to another doctor if your condition is out of their realm of expertise. Still there is One who is without equal, and that is the Great Physician, the Lord Jesus Christ.

The year before we left Susanville I developed a strange tingling sensation on the left side of my face. I had experienced the symptoms in prior years whenever I developed a cold or had allergy attacks. With medication the condition would go away.

This time I went to see my physician and he prescribed antibiotics. There was some relief, but the symptoms persisted. My doctor sent me to another specialist in town and after a brief exam, it was decided that I should see an ear, nose and throat specialist in Reno.

The specialist felt inside of my mouth, and then called his associate into the examination room. He also proceeded to stick his finger in my mouth and feel around inside the lower part of my jaw. There was a definite mass. It was either a tumor, benign or cancerous, or possibly a saliva duct that was blocked. The only way to determine the cause was to perform exploratory surgery. It would be a difficult operation and, should the tumor be malignant, it would be difficult to remove. I could be left with a partial paralysis of the face. Tricia and I prayed, believed, and placed our hands in the Lord's keeping that He would see us through this testing.

Since we lived in Susanville and the operation was to take place in Reno, we were told to check into the hospital the day before. The night I arrived at the hospital my doctor came and assured me all would go well. He related to me that a physician was a fool if he entered into the operating room to perform any type of procedure without the help of God. He felt God was always with him to guide and direct him. Till this day I have the highest regard for Dr. Campolo for he is a man who gives God all the credit and recognizes God is in control.

After the operation, Dr. Campolo: stated that they had found a tumor the size of a dime and that it was not malignant. There is a reason for all things. God used this to prepare me for future ministry. I now can relate and sympathize with those who suffer acute pain.

Chapter Eight

Saying Farewell

We were to leave Susanville in a few months to go on staff in the Western District office of the International Church of the Foursquare Gospel to help establish ethnic churches throughout Northern and Central California, Utah and Northern Nevada.

The next three years of ministry gave us a different perspective on what it means to "go out into all the world and preach the Gospel." We arrived in Modesto, California in July of 1986 with no concept of what it was to help establish ethnic churches. The Lord had given us a strong desire to reach all people. Since I am bilingual speaking Spanish, and English, I felt that at least I had some idea, as to how to evangelize the Hispanic community. Little did I realize the cultural differences that would challenge us and sometimes become stumbling blocks; yet, we accepted our new assignment from God with much anticipation, knowing we were in His will.

Honor Thy Father and Mother

A few months after we arrived in Modesto the Lord called my father home. Dad had suffered a stroke 19 years before, which had left him partially paralyzed and in poor health for several years. He had lost the ability to speak or use his right arm. Dad's greatest frustration was his inability to converse with others. He would become highly agitated because he was unable to put sentences together. When asked a direct question he would respond with a yes or no.

I am forever grateful that my 85-year-old father was a man of great integrity. He was not one who shared his personal life or history, so I know very little of his side of the family. But I do know that he had been abused as a child.

Dad was born in the small fishing village of Truinfo (Triumph) in Baja California, Mexico. He was raised in the state of Sonora,

Mexico and immigrated to this country at the age of seventeen. He had two brothers and three sisters, Dad being the second to the youngest.

My father's mother was a very stern woman. At times she was very abusive to my father, probably due to her being a young widow and having the burden of raising six children on her own. My grandfather died when dad was eleven years old. My father told us that he was used as the scapegoat of the family.

The last time I saw my father's mother alive was in 1947 in Watts, California. Watts in the 30s and 40s was a community of mostly Mexican people and second-generation Mexican-American citizens. We called the area, Chivo Valley, meaning Goat Valley for everyone raised goats and other live stock.

I remember seeing her for the last time as she sat in the sun in an old chair in the back yard of my aunt's home, in front of a little shack. She was unable to speak due to the ravages of a stroke she had suffered a few months prior. It pained me to see this elderly woman who had lived such a harsh life, that all she had to look forward to, was her imminent demise. When I said, "Nana, it's me, Junior," she could not respond for she was unable to recognize me. I don't know if she had a relationship with the Lord when she died a few months later, lonely and broken.

As I reflect about my grandmother and how she lived out her final years at my Tia Cuca's house in Chivo Valley, I am reminded of my aunt Cuca. My aunt, Cuca, was a short, stout woman, with a round red-flushed face who at one time had been a very attractive woman. For some reason my dad had developed a strong relationship with this older sister, the same one who had abused him as a boy.

My aunt was the eldest of my father's brothers and sisters, being ten years older than my father. When the children were young my grandmother worked as a traveling sales woman in Mexico and was gone for weeks at a time. My aunt was forced to be a surrogate mother to my dad and his other brothers and sisters. I loved going to their home to play with all the animals and with my older cousin, Alex.

Alex was later killed in a drive-by killing as he stepped off a street corner. It was a hit and run, not accidental, but retaliation. Tony, Alex's older brother, was one of the leaders of the Watts Pachuco gang and the killing of Alex was in retaliation to Tony.

In the 40's gang members, Pachuco's, were called Zoot Suiters. You could recognize them by the cut of their suits, huge shoulders and large baggy pants, shoes that had soles built up, and wide brimmed flashy hats. They were very striking figures. They were the forerunners of today's Latino gang members.

It was hard for my aunt and her family to deal with the problems that my cousin Tony caused his family. Tony became very militant as a gang member and became a hit man for the Mafia. I later heard that he was serving a life sentence in San Quentin state penitentiary. Paying for his crimes against society and God. How sad that he made such foolish choices.

The memories I have of my father's family and the impact they made on me as an individual became a part of me and helped shape part of my core beliefs, and values. My father was not a religious man nor was a belief in God instilled in me. One of the principles my dad taught me was that if I started something, I had to finish it. He also taught me, never be afraid of hard work and above all else, to be honest in all that I did.

My father's greatest passion in life was baseball. He ate and slept baseball. He seemed to know everything there was to know about the game, but never played it. Before and after World War II he would go to Wrigley field in Los Angeles and Gilmore Stadium in Hollywood to see the Los Angeles Angels or the Hollywood Stars play. Both of these teams were part of the Pacific Coast league, triple A ball clubs. He could tell you every statistic of every player in the entire league. He was a great fan, and in his day, a baseball historian.

It's no wonder I developed a love for the game as a young boy and later played a few years in the minor leagues in the Chicago Cubs farm system. My dad was so proud, that his son was a professional baseball player. My career was cut short due to damage to the rotor cup in my right shoulder. It broke my father's heart when I had to quit playing ball. He seemed to be vicariously living out his dream of playing ball in his son. At 16 years of age, I could "smoke" the baseball, able to throwing the baseball close to 100 miles an hour.

Dad had been hit by a car a few years earlier and, as a result, had a double compound fracture of his right leg. His leg would swell and give him problems. One day while playing catch, Dad told me to "burn" one into his glove. I reared back and let a fast ball fly, and he caught the full force of that fast ball on his bad leg and fell over like a bowling pin. That was the first time I ever saw my father cry. He never blamed me for what happened, but I never threw him another fast ball.

The legacy that my father left me was one of encouragement to do my best. He never interfered with the decisions that I made, whether they were right or wrong. He was always there for me.

Parents are responsible for raising their children and even though your parents, like mine, may not be Christian, they are able to instill strong principles in your life that you will always cherish.

As we prepared to attend my father's funeral in Palm Springs, California, my mind focused on what I was to say at the funeral. Most of my relatives were Roman Catholic, but in name only. As far as I know, my mother was the only "practicing" Catholic in the family. We went directly to my mother's home. I wanted to comfort my Dad's companion and helpmate of 64 years.

The afternoon of the funeral I spoke about how we, his children were the fruit of my father's seed. That our lives would reflect him in all that we did. As I reached the end of the message and eulogy the Lord led me to sing the fifth Psalm. The song ministered to our friends and family but, more importantly, it met the need of the moment, comfort during a time of grief.

The psalmist prayed. "Give ear to my words, O Lord consider my meditation, Hearken unto the voice of my cry, my King and my God; for unto thee will I pray, My voice shalt thou hear in the morning, O Lord in the morning will I direct my prayer unto thee, and will look up" (Psalm 5:1-3 KJV).

I closed the service, and waited until everyone left the sanctuary, then knelt down next to the casket, and wept and sobbed for my father, a man who I respected and honored, a man of great integrity. I had a deep peace in knowing that He was home with Jesus, for my dad had asked Christ to come into his heart a few years prior.

Let me share a few more thoughts regarding my father. His education consisted of a third grade education. He had immigrated to this country at the age of seventeen, and had a deep respect for the laws of the land and the laws of God. I am privileged to carry his name.

Fifteen months after my father's death we received a call that mom had passed away. Mother's funeral was not as difficult to officiate as was my fathers, but being the oldest son and a minister, my brothers and sisters leaned on me for spiritual strength.

God's people are used as His emissaries to help bring peace to those who are hurting emotionally and His peace as He promised in His word. There is no set formula to minister comfort in times of sorrow. It is God the Holy Spirit, who gives proper words to say to those who are in pain. My family was in pain. God used me to bring comfort to them.

None of us know what is going through a person's heart in times of pain and anguish; we can only surmise how one feels. We need to listen to those who are suffering, then respond to their specific need. For some a pat on the back or a touch on the shoulder may bring comfort. For others crying helps ease the pain.

Always pray in a crisis situation that those involved would experience peace. People often look to believers for strength in times of sorrow and grief. Most people can tell when you are sincere and truly care. The Lord of the church will always be there for us in times of trial. "I will never desert you, nor will I forsake you" (Heb. 13:5).

One of the processes of life we all must confront is the demise of the family. When parents die generally the siblings loose the closeness of the other family members. Parents are the "tie that binds." God has ordered the human cycle of life.

When couples have children they start their own families. The bonding of each member of the family takes place within this structure. Each of the siblings, for some reason, will bond closer to one of the other siblings. This bonding will last all their lives.

I believe that God allows this process in order for us to cope in times of trial. We will gravitate to the brother or sister who we bonded with in our formative years. This process happens in all families unless there is only one child, then that child seeks fusion with a near relative. Every family, with a few exceptions, must experience this course. When this process does not take place we feel lost without it. This process is called bonding.

My mother's death brought the demise or end of my family, as we had known it for so many years. God, in time, would fill the void during the mourning process. We are left with the fond memories of joy and sorrow that we experienced as children, but when we leave the nest and start our own family, the process of family starts all over again. It is an on-going phenomenon that will continue until the Lord returns.

The last nineteen years of my mother's life were devoted to caring for every need of my father. When my father went to be with the Lord mother gave up her will to live. She had been a devoted, faithful wife for so many years. Now she had lost her best friend and companion. Truly they were one. I can still hear her last words, not of despair, but of a deep desire to be with dad and Jesus.

God, in taking her home, eased her pain, of sorrow and grief. Emotional pain is one of the common realities of life. But we can stand firm in knowing that scripture comforts us. "He shall wipe away every tear from their eyes; and there shall no longer be any death; there shall no longer be any mourning, or crying, or pain; the first things have passed away" (Rev. 21:4).

My mother lived 84 years, 64 of them were spent married to my father. She bore my father nine children, of which I am the fourth, and the eldest son. She had a deep commitment to Jesus and an inner strength that came from her relationship with Him.

The death of both of my parents left me with a sense of detachment to this world. But I am left with an assurance that I will see them again in my heavenly Father's mansion. Sorrow is for a moment and soon passes with time, but God is eternal, and His eternal realm is waiting for us in the next life. This is every believer's hope.

I can still see both of my parents in my memories. These are great memories of times past. One of the fondest memories I have of my early years was walking into my mother's kitchen and seeing her preparing my father's evening meal. It consisted of fresh baked tortillas, a piece of deep fried beef steak, topped with a large plate of refried beans, rice and a cup of extra strong black coffee. Topped off, with a little canned milk, added for flavor. I have other memories just as vivid, but I remember that my mother's life was spent serving God, her husband, and her children in that order.

Both my parents left me with a great legacy of values, honesty and integrity. They had very little education, but they were wise in what they taught us. They lived what they taught. Neither one went any higher in their education than the fifth grade, but they were blessed with good common sense. I am grateful to God that He instilled these values in my parents.

Make Disciples of All the Nations

Working in the Western District office was a great learning experience for us. God used us to help establish ethnic churches within the district. We met numerous new friends from different cultures and languages. Christian friendships that we both treasure. We experienced some disappointments, but generally we were blessed in doing what God had called us to do. We traveled many miles throughout the district, completely wearing out a small vehicle, but it was worth the time and commitment for we saw God's hand in all our endeavors.

We had a wonderful time reaching people, of various cultures and languages for Christ. Most of the pastors we assisted in the Western District had to be bi-vocational. It troubled us to see the price these men and women had to pay in order to serve God. They are truly blessed of the Lord.

We were to stay in Modesto for almost three years and in December of 1989 we were asked to accept the pastorate in the Oroville, California, Foursquare Church. We accepted the pastorate in Oroville, we did so with a sense of anxiety. I believe the Holy Spirit was teaching me something, so I simply obeyed the leading of the Lord, not knowing what awaited us.

As far as I am concerned the highest call an individual can receive from God, is to be a pastor. With this call there will be times of rejection by well meaning saints. The hardest challenge to a minister is not to be confrontational with people. Oroville would be such a challenge. I am grateful that God called us to this community for a season. It was to be a great learning experience for us. The anxiety I felt in my spirit was what awaited me, but His grace gave us strength to meet every challenge we would encounter.

We continued to serve as overseers of the ethnic churches, while pastoring in Oroville, and in August of 1999 we resigned as overseers to ethnic pastors due to the many responsibilities we currently have.

Chapter Nine

God Sent Me To Build Up Not Tear Down

Oroville, California, a community made up mostly of retired people is located northeast of Sacramento. The town has approximately 14,000 inhabitants, while the greater area encompasses roughly 55,000 souls. Chico is located 25 miles away. The area is rich in agriculture, but is better known for its lake and dam. Which attracts many tourists to the area for fishing and camping.

When I accepted the Oroville pastorate I almost wept, and had such a horrible feeling in my stomach that I almost became sick. Little did we know what awaited us in this church? We were about to find out.

The problem surfaced shortly after we arrived. We learned that there were some deep-rooted hurts, which were based on church ideologies. The church had been birthed from a split of another congregation, which had a congregational structure. This meant that when a pastoral change is necessary; the new pastor is chosen by a majority vote of membership.

Our denominational polity is a modified Episcopal, model, pastors are appointed by a District Supervisor with the approval of the International Board. The problem manifested itself, when the District Supervisor, rather than being voted on by the congregation appointed us. The problem was compounded by the abrupt resignation of the previous pastor, which caused many hurts and ill feelings among the parishioners. I sympathized with them about their having no voice in the selection process of their pastor, convictions that were based on their ecclesiology.

When the former pastor left; the congregation was unprepared by the change and felt betrayed. Others were angry and deeply pained emotionally. Some were left with a deep mistrust of denominations while others lost confidence in pastors. I became aware of their feelings the second month we were there. Unfortunately, a

61

handful vented their frustrations on Tricia and me. We were deeply wounded by a handful of bitter, wounded Christians.

While speaking from the pulpit in this church, instead of a sense of joy and acceptance, I experienced hostility. As a Christian leader I had never experienced such rejection from other brothers and sisters in Christ.

After a year the handful of disgruntled people left the church. Unfortunately they took their guile and attitudes with them and practiced their brand of Christianity on another congregation and pastor.

As humans it is very difficult for us to love people who vent their frustrations against us. I cried and prayed for these poor misguided souls. One thing we learned was not to retaliate, but try to see others as God views them. Trying to teach kingdom principles to bruised souls was an important lesson for both of us. It was awkward for me to look at these souls each time we gathered and love them in spite of their actions. We felt betrayed and deeply pained in our hearts. We had gone there to love and nurture the people, but the feelings of rejection became a daily occurrence and started to take their toll on my health.

I was also accused of manipulating the church funds and using the money for personal use. A letter was sent to the Western District Supervisor regarding the allegations. We had to answer the charges, which were all proven false. This added to my feelings of rejection and anguish. Though we were exonerated of these charges, the damage had been done to us in the community. My character had been slandered and therefore, we were hindered in reaching others with the Gospel.

The Lord showed me a Christian principle during this difficult time in ministry rather than retaliate, turn the other cheek. Never lower yourself to the level of your persecutors by expressing your anger toward them. Always keep your composure and above all, pray for them. These people were not my enemies, nor were they simply out to destroy me. They were wounded and blinded by their hurts. I could no more demand that they stop their accusations than I could force them to submit to me as their shepherd. Paul writes,

"Now I urge you, brethren, keep your eye on those who cause dissension and hindrances contrary to the teaching which you learned, and turn away from them. For such men are slaves not of our Lord Christ, but of there own appetites; and by their smooth and flattering speech they deceive the hearts of the unsuspecting" (Rom. 16:17-18).

Though I am a Christian pastor, it was extremely difficult for me not to return evil for evil, but I felt if I served Christ and Him only, then He would exonerate me. If I am to survive as a minister, I must live by His word. The Bible states, "And we know that God causes all things to work together for good to those who love God, to those who are called according to His purpose" (Rom. 8:28). Today I can look back and thank Him for sending us to Oroville.

Over the years I have met and conversed at length with men and women who were called into full time ministry. The heartaches that they had experienced we also have suffered. Rejection is so cruel and harsh that many good and decent young men and women have left the ministry because of it.

One of the hallmarks of true Christianity is unity. But when well meaning church members insist on having there own way, in violation of God's word, the church becomes vulnerable to criticism from the secular world. If we are divisive and argumentative we destroy one another. Jesus said, "A house divided against itself falls" (Luke 11:17b). Those who are forced to choose sides or those who leave the church also suffer. Many leave the fellowship and ultimately become bitter after losing touch with healthy Christians.

Because the church is to model the life of Christ and His teaching's, we discredit Him when we allow our personal likes and dislikes to rule our hearts. Jesus said, "A new commandment I give you, that you love one another, even as I have loved you, that you also love one another. By this all men will know that you are My disciples, if you have love for one another" (John 13:33-34). When people are divisive they tear each other apart instead of loving one another as Christ loves us. As we put aside our selfish desires and place Christ first we fulfill His new commandment.

Christ Gave Us the Ministry of Reconciliation

Restoration and reconciliation are terms used in Christianity for those who have lost fellowship with Christ. But those who have been wounded by others who were selfish and insensitive also need help. One of the roles of the church is to bring healing to the suffering. Rejection often causes tremendous pain.

Pastors are to be treated with love like other members of the body of Christ. Paul writes, "Let the elders who rule well be considered worthy of double honor, especially those who work hard at preaching and teaching" (1 Tim.5:17). Pastors are to receive "double honor," yet there are those who have a different view. I believe that there is no higher call in life than to serve in the pastorate. We must strive to help each pastor achieve their potential in Christ by being sensitive to their emotional and physical needs, especially for those who are self-supporting. Not enough is being done for those who have been hurt in ministry. The books that have been written concerning ministry burnout can be a great asset and help for guidance, but they are not enough to restore and help pastors who are going through difficult times.

Every Christian organization should have qualified counselors trained for the express purpose of making sure that their ministers are well taken care of emotionally. We do them an injustice if we don't provide such help in times of emotional stress. Pastors become more vulnerable to temptations, which can cause them to fall into self- destructive patterns of sin.

Pastoral burnout is real and not to be taken lightly. We should all take time off for recreation, good regimented exercise, plenty of rest and sleep, plus a good healthy diet. We need a confidant, or mentor, that we can relate our feelings to in times of emotional stress. Rather than our spouse, this should be someone of the same sex, perhaps an older pastor or close friend. Times of solitude in prayer with the Lord are a great help. Hobbies are a must. A pastor should never forget that his/her spouse often shares the same feelings. They also need to be ministered to. Ministers should always forgive those who are insensitive to them while remembering the words of our Lord; "Father forgive them; for they do not know what they are doing" (Luke 23:34a).

64

While we were in Oroville I needed to find secular work since the income of the church was not enough to support us and pay a sizable mortgage payment. I went to work for the Mental Health Department of Butte County as a mental health counselor. God took a situation of dissension and divisiveness in His body and turned it into a blessing for me and for His glory. "Trust in the Lord with all your heart, and do not lean on your own understanding" (Prov. 3:6).

My job entailed working on three different school campuses, counseling youth from six years to nineteen years of age and their families. I was the only Bilingual Spanish speaking counselor in the county. The youth that I counseled were considered at risk, because of emotional problems. They were either from dysfunctional homes or had been abused physically or sexually. I also worked with youth gangs and those suffering from drug and alcohol addiction.

I saw so much pain, anger, frustration and rejection each day that at times it was difficult for me to unwind when I arrived home. All this stress was compounded by what we were experiencing in the church. It was only God's grace and mercy that sustained me and gave me the will to continue. Because of the pressures and the problems of the church and trying to help the young people whose lives were being torn apart each day, I found myself weeping as I dealt with many young people whose lives were being shattered. Our greatest resource is our children, yet they are often torn apart by insensitive, selfish parents who place themselves, rather than their children first.

There were hundreds of young people whose lives I was able to influence in some small way, but it would take a volume to write them all down. Many of those with whom I came in contact, left me with a feeling of anger because of the abuse that I knew had been inflicted upon them. These children were scarred for life due to their home situations and environment.

Chapter Ten

Suffer The Little Children

Child abuse is rampant in our society today and unless we deal with the reason for it, we will continue to reap its ill effects for generations to come. Most child abuse is not sexual or physical, but emotional.

Behavioral science states that behavior patterns are learned, impacted by our social environment and culture. We are predisposed to certain inherited characteristics, but generally we are what we have been taught. Behavior is first introduced to the child by his home environment. It is enhanced in the school, either positively or negatively. When the child interacts with others during the formative years he/she is learning certain behavior patterns. What the child sees and hears will become part of him.

Jesus addressed child abuse when He stated. "But whoever causes one of these little ones who believe in Me to stumble, it is better for him that a heavy millstone be hung around his neck, and that he be drowned in the depth of the sea" (Matt. 18:6). Our children become what they are taught.

One of the most tragic situations that I encountered dealt with a young child of six. The school principle asked me if I would please speak with this child because of some of her behavioral problems. The school principle was a very compassionate woman and a believer. I had developed a good working relationship with her and her staff.

I remember the day that this child was brought to my office. I was at this particular school three hours a week. I could have spent fifteen hours a week in this school alone. She came to my office dressed in a little cotton dress. The shortness of her sleeves showed that it was obviously much too small for her. She had a habit of constantly pulling on the sleeves of her dress. I imagined this was her only dress. She sat down in front of me at a little child's table. I felt very awkward sitting in such a small chair, due to my size.

She was very open with me as we talked, but I noticed a deep sadness to her demeanor, especially when she started to relate to me what had happened to her.

Without any prompting from me, she proceeded to tell me a nightmarish story. Her fears were based on a frightening experience. She and her siblings had been taken to the police station. She related that her daddy had left them in a motel room and had gone for pizza and some diapers for two of the other children. This traumatic incident had occurred in a run down part of San Diego. She had been frightened by the men in uniform and the flashing lights of the squad cars outside the room. The children were taken to the county juvenile detention facility to wait for her daddy's return. I asked her when all this had taken place? She replied that it was a couple of week's ago. We talked for a little while longer and then, like most children her age, her retention span was broken. I then sent her back to her class. As we talked it was hard for me to restrain my tears.

Though I had other counseling sessions with this child, this particular day will always be etched in my memory. My paternal instinct was to hug her and tell her how much Jesus loved her, but because of current restrictive laws, to do so would be construed as child abuse, all I could do was pray for God's love to be showered on her.

Afterwards I was told when all this had taken place. Although the incident she had related me about was real, it had occurred nine months prior. Her mother a drug addict had deserted them. The father, a recovering addict, was trying to find work. He had left the children in a run down motel in a hard core area of San Diego alone and without any food. He had left this older child in charge of the younger children, while he sought help.

This child had been so traumatized by her experience that she could not distinguish reality. My role was a positive one in this child's life. I did manage to instill in her that what she had experienced was real, but that that it was in the past. She was reliving this incident each day of her life. This child and her siblings were the real victims. I wish I could tell you that this story had a happy ending but, unfortunately, it did not. Her uncle took them in for awhile while the father sought work.

This child was scarred for life and will always have bad dreams about that night. I often wondered about her brothers and sisters and how badly where they affected. This child will suffer self-esteem problems the rest of her life. This traumatic night will became a vivid memory, but added to it are the memories of a broken childhood. A mother who deserted her who later died of an overdose of heroin.

The chances of this child growing up to become a productive mature woman are slim, because of her early formative years. Based on behavioral patterns she will likely follow in her parent's footsteps. This is a real tragedy that our society has not grasped, the reality that unless our morals change, we are doomed as a nation. Moses warned the Israelites that God would "visit the iniquity of the fathers on the children and on the grandchildren to the third and fourth generations of those who hate Me, but showing lovingkindness to thousands, to those who love Me and keep my commandments" (Exodus 20:5-6). Children are being made to pass through the fire because of the sins of the fathers. Thank God that our Lord is a loving and compassionate creator that forgives our inequities and that each one is held accountable for there own transgressions.

Since I worked for a county agency and in the public schools, I was not allowed to preach or initiate any thing having to due with religion. Most of those I worked with and those I counseled knew that I was a pastor. I had many opportunities to share Christ.

Don't Let the Sun Go Down on Your Wrath
One emotion exhibited by youth from dysfunctional families is anger. Almost all of those I counseled with expressed differing degrees of anger brought on by feelings of rejection. In most cases this ire is brought on by family situations. Without exception each child and teenager expressed feelings of guilt, rejection and anger. In some, their anger became wrathful and expressed itself by unruly behavior.

69

One case in particular was the tragic plight of a young woman I will call Sally. My contact person at this particular high school asked me if I would take her as a client. Her lamentable tale was that her parents had belonged to a notorious biker gang and both were heavy drug users. The mother had died of an overdose of heroin and the father was still using drugs. He was trying to make a home for the girl, but was having difficulty staying drug free and holding down a job.

Sally confided to me that she had been sexually molested and abused by friends of her parent's. She had been introduced to street drugs at the age of nine and later became addicted. She had been exposed to every form of sexual deviation known to man, and besides all this, she had been physically abused and, at times, knocked unconscious by the beatings inflicted upon her.

To add to this scenario, Sally was also suicidal and, in the course of several counseling sessions, expressed to me that she was having an affair with a twenty two year old woman. During the weeks that followed, I noticed that she was showing early stages of paranoid schizophrenia. In one of our sessions she confided that she was hearing voices. During most of our sessions she was extremely agitated. It seemed that she was a time bomb ready to explode.

One afternoon she came to my office and asked if she could talk with me so I gave her a pass to leave her class. I could see that her agitation had grown worse. In our conversation she related to me that she was contemplating taking her own life. My reaction was not of surprise, but of compassion. The reason I was not surprised was that in the course of a year I had dealt with over fifty suicidal youth. My concern was that she would carry out her threat. I tried to get her to sign a suicide contract with me. These contracts help a counselor bond with a suicidal person especially a youth. The rules of the contract stated that she would not try to take her life without first talking with another crisis worker or me. The rules also stated that if the client refused to sign the agreement the county authorities would be notified and the client would be placed in the mental health ward for observation and their own protection.

She refused to sign the contract and since I had no choice, I called the police department and they came and took her away.

Before the police arrived I asked her why she had become so distraught that she wanted to end her life and her response shocked me. She was in a rage because her lover had rejected her and had left her for another person. Her anger was not so much that her lover had left her, but that she had left her for a man. She could not deal with the idea that her former lover was bisexual. This sent Sally into a rage. All the twisted emotional abuses that this child had endured in her formative years had finally come to a climax. Her mind could not comprehend reality and something inside her snapped.

When they were placing her into the squad car to take her to the county mental ward, she asked me if I would come and visit her. I later went to visit her in the mental health unit and reassured her that what was happening to her was for her best interest. She was much calmer due to the medications they had given her.

I had an opportunity to share the gospel with her and tell her how much Jesus loved her, that if she would give her heart to Him, she would find peace. She was not very responsive to what I shared and shortly after this encounter I left. It would be the last time I had contact with Sally, a girl of fifteen, old beyond her years. I have often thought of her, as to her plight in life, but more important her soul.

This scenario is one of the most tragic incidents that I have encountered. What about the other Sally's of this world? I openly wept for this child and others who have suffered the same plight. We must keep in focus what a godless society can produce. We as Christians are responsible for our children and for what type of individuals they become in the way we raise them. Paul writes, "And, fathers, do not provoke your children to anger; but bring them up in the discipline and instruction of the Lord" (Eph. 6:4). The parents of this girl were the culprits for her plight; they must answer to God for the way they abused her and raised her. She will give account to God for her actions.

Are we as a Judeo-Christian nation and society held to a higher standard by God in maintaining a moral social structure to protect our children? I think so.

The mind in its formative years can be programmed for either good or bad by what it is exposed to. Our emotions are God given. Feelings of despair, rejection, anxiety and the other emotions that distinguish us from the animal world are affected by how we are treated by our parents. Sally was truly a victim; she became what she had learned as a small child.

What did I, as a minister and Christian, learn from the life of this young woman? I learned that all life is precious in the sight of God and that I should be more compassionate to lonely rejected children, whose self worth and self esteem have been shattered by insensitive people who make life difficult.

One case that came to my attention had to do with incest, which is strictly forbidden by God. "No one is to approach any close relative to have sexual relations. I am the Lord" (Lev. 18:6). The case had to do with the family of a young man whose father was convicted of molesting his older sisters.

Roberto (not actual name) was born with a health condition that made it difficult for him to participate in school sports of any type. It is amazing that he was able to walk, but despite his handicap, he was able to play football and other sports.

I was asked to counsel him because of his anger and hostility exhibited towards others. His personality had changed drastically because of his father's molestation of his sisters. The father had been convicted and sentenced to prison for his actions. Roberto vented his anger by constantly getting into brawls with his schoolmates and, at times, being disrespectful of his teachers.

My first encounter with Roberto was very cordial. I felt I had made a good impression on him and that he trusted me to some extent. He was however in total denial of his father's actions. As we conversed, he related to me what a great dad his father had been to him and his brothers and sisters. He could not come to grips with the reality that his father, whom he truly loved, would do such a thing.

I later met with his two younger brothers and their mother. The sisters were both taken from the home and placed in foster homes. I met with each one on an individual basis, as well as with the family once a week. The whole family had been devastated by the father's actions. He had been sentenced to 12 years in a state prison for the acts he had perpetrated upon each of his two daughters. He not only had committed these heinous crimes against his daughters, but he had also defiled the marriage bed and defamed his sons by his horrific actions.

Each member of this family had been scarred for life and would need counseling for many months to come. The wife and mother of the children found that her life had suddenly and drastically changed. She had been thrust into a situation that she was unable to cope with emotionally. Her marriage was shattered, and her sons and daughters were divided as to who they would believe.

The daughters were taken from the home and placed in foster care for a short period of time. Later both girls left their foster homes and became very promiscuous. The youngest girl was impacted the most; going from one relationship to another, seeking the love her father had robbed her of. The family unit had been destroyed. This all happened because of the actions of the husband and father.

I never met the father; but justice was done according to God's word. "Everyone who does any of these detestable things-such persons must be cut off from their people" (Lev. 18:29). As far as I know he is still in prison.

Sex within the bounds of marriage is ordained by God and is a healthy wholesome act. Incest goes against all that is decent and honorable and is as God say's, an abomination. Those who perpetrate the act of incest must pay the penalty to the state and God will also judge them.

Family members who have been devastated by incest generally have a life long hatred and anger against the person who actuates the crime. Core beliefs regarding sex within the confines of marriage become twisted and warped. Some incest victims are so affected that they seek same sex partners and many become sex offenders themselves. Some of the young women who have been abused develop eating disorders and other emotional problems.

In most cases the offender was abused in their childhood. Molestation and incest is a learned behavior, and recovery is almost non-existent. Many of our state institutions are overflowing with pedophiles that have committed sexual offenses against young innocent victims. These men have become predators who prey on the innocent. All offenders are constantly in denial. They live with deep feelings of guilt and the constant fear of exposure, fearing that others will know their hidden secret and that they will be exposed for their crimes.

They convince themselves that they too are victims. The predator rationalizes his behavior and justifies his actions by blaming the victim. This then enables him to continue to prey on others. What a tragedy!

We live in a selfish world and because it is self-seeking we are slowly destroying our youth. We are consumed with our own feelings and self-interests. Secularists believe that the damage we are doing to our children is irreversible. Paul writes, "Or do you not know that the unrighteous shall not inherit the kingdom of God? Do not be deceived; neither fornicators, nor adulterers, nor effeminate, nor homosexuals, nor thieves, nor the covetous, nor drunkards, nor revilers, nor swindlers, shall inherit the kingdom of God. And such were some of you; but you were washed, but you were sanctified, but you were justified in the name of Christ, and in the Spirit of our God" (1Cor. 6:9-11). When Paul said "and such were some of you," his inference was that some of them had committed various sexual sins, but they had been washed by the blood of the Lamb. God always extends mercy to those who repent of their actions. There is hope for all the victims as well as the perpetrators.

Teach Them to Fear the Lord

At one of the schools I served there were several gang members. Most of them were mainly Latino. I conducted group therapy for four groups of these gang members, male and female.

When I first arrived on campus I was met with much suspicion. The kids thought I was a narcotics officer. There were plenty of drugs to purchase on the school grounds, so any new staff member was scrutinized very closely. It took about two months for the students to accept me. But once they knew they could trust me, I became a confidant. The wild stories and the violence that they

74

were exposed to daily only made me more compassionate in my dealings with them.

Some of the girls became pregnant and a few talked about abortion. I was able to convince a few of them to give their babies up for adoption. Though there are many other issues that gang members feel are important to them, the most important issue for all of them was being accepted and accepted by their peers.

I learned that gang members place great importance on what is happening at any given moment. As I became a better listener I was able to pick up information when there was going to be a gang confrontation.

Tricia and I were asked to chaperone the "Senior Latino Dance." The night of the dance I overheard a conversation relative to a fight that was going to be outside the school gym. I rounded up one of my helpers and went outside. There were over three hundred youth, mostly gang members, in a confrontation with a handful of African American kids from another town. One of the black kids pulled out a shotgun and was about to use it to defend himself. I strode through the middle of this confrontation and calmed the crisis. I took the gun away from the young man and told him to put it in the trunk of the car and leave. Though he did as he was told the situation was still very volatile. When they saw me coming they parted because they respected my judgement and knew I was a man of God. I later found out that many of the youth had all sorts of weapons and that we could have had a horrible tragedy if I hadn't taken action.

I was given a nickname, "Spider," as youngster. It was the name I used when I was part of a gang. A guy named Ralph had tagged me with this moniker and when the kids at this school found this out, they started calling me "Spider." This was a term of affection, and to them I was never Mr. Contreras, but considered one of them.

Some of these kids had never traveled further than Sacramento. Many of them had very little communication with their fathers, so when I decided to take them to Modesto, for the "American Graffiti Nights," a yearly celebration taken from the movie by the same name, they were ecstatic. Transportation to the event was a problem, but we managed to get them all into our two vehicles. Tricia had our small car packed full of male gang members and I drove a van with the rest of the young men. I told them they were going to have to be on their best behavior and they did not disappoint us. Those young men still talk about that night when we went to Modesto to the big street cruise.

I showed these young men and women that Christ cared for them through my actions. They repaid me in kind by inviting me to their high school graduation. They called me to come from Salinas, Ca, and attend. What an honor to see the fruit of our labors. All of them were potential high school dropouts when we first met. I was never so proud of a group of kids who stayed in school because of what we had accomplished together. Occasionally I still hear from some of them.

Before I Formed You in the Womb I Knew You

Emotional illness in the last three and a half decades has exploded. There are more people with bipolar diseases today than ever before. Schizophrenia and manic-depression are the two most common. Why is this? I believe many young people today could become full-fledged manic-depressives and schizophrenics. Rejection is the main cause for many with diagnosed bipolar problems. Anger and guilt is the fruit of rejection. These emotions should be dealt with when a person is young. Individuals who manifest some of the symptoms can be a walking "time bomb," ready to explode.

My conviction about this is based on sound research. In working with the emotionally disturbed youth with bipolar illnesses, I found that they all had two things in common, anger and rejection.

Rejection or acceptance starts in the womb at conception. In counseling sessions often they relate feelings of despair and loneliness. They feel detached from their mothers because of a lack of bonding. To them all of these feelings are real. Others feel that they were never allowed to express their feelings, especially in their formative years. A large percentage of these people come from broken homes, with feelings of detachment and not being loved.

Bonding takes place at conception in the womb. The mother's attitude will influence the emotional health of the infant. Studies have been done as to the feelings that the infant senses while in the womb. Luke relates that when Mary went to visit Elizabeth, the

76

mother of "John the Baptist," a unique incident happened. "When Elizabeth heard Mary's greeting the baby leaped in her womb; and Elizabeth was filled with the Holy Spirit. And she cried with a loud voice, and said 'Blessed among women are you, and blessed is the fruit of your womb! And how has it happened to me that the mother of my Lord should come to me? For behold, when the sound of your greeting reached my ears, the baby leaped in my womb for joy'" (Luke 1:41-44). This is proof that all babies can feel joy, sorrow and love.

Love is part of the bonding process. It starts in the womb. When love is denied an infant during its formative period, chances are the individual will have emotional problems as an adult or even younger.

"Crack" babies are an example of this process. They are taken from the mother and placed in foster homes, thus breaking the bond. Often they are placed in natal intensive care units in order to detoxify them. Bonding in most cases is denied, due to the care they require. Some are mentally underdeveloped and will be retarded children.

A child of rape or incest can experience these same feelings. They usually have little self-esteem and have difficulty relating to their peers.

Where is the father in all this? The mother's love and bonding is extremely critical during the first six months of the child's rearing. The father bonds to the child during its formative years, from infancy to its eighth year. Both parents will influence the individual the rest of their lives. John the Baptist is a great example, his father having played a vital role in his life.

Rejection can give birth to selfishness. When God rejected Cain's offering, the Lord said, "Why are you angry? And why has your countenance fallen?" (Gen. 4:6). Cain later killed his brother though God had warned him to deal with his anger. "Sin is crouching at your door; and it's desire is for you, but you must master it" (Gen. 4:7b). Cain's rejection came from a selfish motive. Most of us learn to cope with rejection, but those with deep-rooted emotional problems find it extremely difficult. People with bipolar illnesses feel rejected when they are very young. They do not feel wanted because they lack the one thing they want the most, love.

What can be done for these poor souls who feel unloved? Secular society often masks the problem by mind-altering drugs, without dealing with the real problem. The individuals they are trying to help lack love and acceptance.

Most of the homeless people wandering the streets have mental illnesses. They belong in controlled environments. What is the role of the church in helping them find rest for their tormented minds? There are very few qualified counselors trained to help people with mental illness. As Christians, it is imperative that we develop ministries that can help people cope with their illness. Our seminaries and Bible colleges are way behind in this area.

Jesus dealt with a man who was demon possessed who, the Bible says, was "constantly night and day, among the tombs and in the mountains, he was crying out and gashing himself with the stones. And seeing Jesus from a distance, he ran up and bowed down before Him" (Mark 5:5-6). Jesus felt compassion for the man. He dealt with the immediate problem. He delivered the man from the agony of demonic possession. He was an outcast shunned by his people. The Torah stated that he had to be separated from society. The great Rabbi, Jesus, went against the law. He spoke kindness and love to the man. We are called to do the same. The man was separated from his people because of his affliction: Jesus restored him and freed him from bondage. When we accept Christ as our Lord and Savior we are bonded to Him. Only Christ can restore and make whole.

Jesus felt rejection when He cried, "My God, My God why have you forsaken Me?" (Mark 15:34). Jesus felt rejection from the Father. If He felt this separation from the Father, alone and in agony, it's no wonder people with mental disorders feel the same. Jesus was an example on reaching those who are hurting; we are to do the same.

The youth that I have dealt with have left me with a greater awareness for the need to save our marriages and thus stop the destruction of our youth. Josh McDowell in his book "Right from Wrong" stated some frightening statistics about our youth, not "other people's children," but "church youth," youth that do not see a standard of truth in their parents. "The reason, then, that youth who do not accept objective truth are more likely to lie, cheat, or get drunk, is that they are seeing their choices through faulty lenses. They have embraced a world-view about truth that blinds them to the difference between right and wrong. The difference between the counterfeits and the real thing." We are told that 36 percent of our youth are likely to lie to their parents; that 48 percent cheat on school examines and that 74 percent watch MTV, a TV net work that shows sex, violence, perversion and rebellion against society.

These staggering figures should give us a wakeup call, but the greater culprit is divorce and separation of the family structure. The number one cause of mental illness, crime and violence, promiscuous sex, rape, incest, drug and alcohol abuse among Americas youth, is the break up of the family.

For some we will be the only "Jesus" that they will ever know. How we Christians live as examples will affect our youth, in a positive or negative way.

Oroville was to be a place where I came of age as a Christian. I was exposed to what life is all about in ministry. God let me see through His eyes for a moment in time. What I learned and felt was real. We must strive to always preach the truth. That Christ wants to restore people to wholeness. As Christians we are living proof of what God can do. The real challenge is to sense the leading of the Holy Spirit. His word is truth and can bring healing to the hurting soul. God uses trial and error in our lives to show us Kingdom principles, so we in turn can minister to others. "Blessed be the God and Father of our Lord Jesus Christ, the Father of mercies and God of all comfort" (2Cor 1:3). We are called to comfort others.

Chapter Eleven

Praying For The Sick

I accepted the Chaplaincy of Natividad Medical Facility in the fall of 1994 and officially started my duties December of that year. There are many misconceptions about the duties and responsibilities of a hospital chaplain. I have some strong views concerning my role at the hospital and the impact that I have on all the physicians, nurses, staff, patients and volunteers.

First and foremost I consider myself an ambassador of Christ. Paul writes, "Therefore, we are ambassadors for Christ, as though God were entreating through us" (2Cor.5). In other words, I represent Christ as His ambassador, and must reflect Him in my treatment of each and every person. I am to love them and minister to their needs. I am not at the hospital to judge, to condemn, or to espouse a cause or a doctrine. I believe the best way to direct souls to Jesus is to first love them as He loves me and let them see Christ in me. If the Lord opens doors for me to witness His plan of salvation, then I will respond with the Gospel.

I have had the opportunity to pray for people of different faiths, but always in the name of the Lord. I have been privileged to pray for two elderly Jewish patients who were victims of the Nazi holocaust. Both were women in there nineties, one a German Jew, the other a Russian Jew. Although I was not able to communicate to these two precious souls in their respective tongues, I was able to witness to each of them by praying for them in the name of the Lord. I was also able to minister to their families as well.

Once I prayed for an Egyptian gentleman who was terminally ill due to kidney failure. I introduced myself to him, told him who I was and asked if he would allow me to pray for him. He shared with me that he was of the Muslin faith, but it was fine with him. Moslems believe that Christ was a prophet, so for him, he felt blessed that I would pray for him. He died a few weeks later, but during his short stay at the hospital, I was able to pray for him several times. The sad part of this scenario was that because of his religious beliefs, he refused to go on dialysis, which would have prolonged his life. I prayed for physical healing and even shared the good news with him, but his heart was hardened and could not spiritually accept my beliefs. He chose to die according to his beliefs. It was his choice and in the end he would have to answer to God.

I know that when people are sick they need a touch from God, so each time I walk into a room I ask myself, how would Jesus approach this patient. This is my philosophy. As I talk with them or extend a brief God bless you, this helps ease the pain for many. I never impose myself on any patient when I enter a room. I introduce myself as the hospital chaplain and state that I am a Christian.

I have been blessed time and time again by being available at all times. I have lost a lot of sleep and at times wondered why God called me to this ministry. Each day brings a new challenge, but always an opportunity to share the good news.

You Shall Know Them by Their Fruit

Once a local newspaper interviewed me as to my role as chaplain. The reporter asked why I wore a clergy collar since I was a Protestant minister. I wear it because it serves a purpose. First: it identifies me as being a clergyman. It also makes me aware of how people react to a minister or priest. As a doctor wears a white frock coat, the collar sets me apart from other hospital personnel. Each day I put on the shirt with the special collar, I ask the Lord to watch over me so that my actions would not dishonor Him.

The role of the chaplain is to be a spiritual guide and leader to the staff, patients and volunteers. There have been times when a doctor, a nurse, or staff person has asked for counsel, or for prayer. Others simply want me to be there for them through a stressful time. Some ask counsel for marital problems, others in dealing with their children. I also get numerous questions about the Bible and spiritual matters.

Certain days are very stressful and there are times that I feel very inadequate. Regardless of the circumstance, His word sustains me. "I can do all things through Him who strengthens me" (Phil. 4:13).

Many times my beeper will go off even before I walk through the front door of the hospital and I am confronted with a crisis situation. I go prepared no matter what the situation may be.

I the Lord Am Your Healer

Once I was asked to visit a young man who had the advanced stages of AIDS. He asked if I would pray for him. The tragedy and waste was evident for here was a man in his middle thirties dying of this dreaded disease. His eminent demise could have been avoided if he had lived a different life style. His live-in partner, sitting at his bedside, looked and acted like a woman. He was waiting for a sex change operation. He was willing to mutilate his body to please his partner. My heart ached when this story unfolded. The young man would eventually succumb because he bought a lie, the lie that claims God, had made him that way. He told me that I was one of the few clergy that would even talk to him. I did not sit in judgment on this man for only God can judge, but I do not have to buy into the deception that claims God created homosexuals.

Paul in writing to the church at Corinth reminds them that they had lived abhorrent life styles. "But you were washed, but you were sanctified, but you were justified in the name of the Lord Jesus Christ" (1Cor. 6:11). The young man also told me that he had a wife and children. He would not elaborate as to why his marriage failed, but I could see how warped his thinking was.

If some humans are born as homosexuals, then everything that I hold sacred and believe that the Bible states is a lie. If the Bible is not the word of God then every person I have ever witnessed too has been told a falsehood and is dead in their trespasses. I know from my own testimony that God is real. I have seen far too many convincing proofs that He is real and that His word is truth. As a Christian and an ambassador for Christ I can only pray for the souls of these two young men. The man with the terminal illness later succumbed to the ravages of AIDS.

This same day I was asked to report to the special section that is set aside for the inmates from Soledad prison. A prisoner had requested to see me, and was about to undergo a surgical procedure to remove an obstruction lodged in his esophagus. The almost humorous aspect of this needless surgery was that this man had had twenty-seven previous surgeries to remove objects that he has swallowed. Over the years he had ingested various metal and plastic objects, such as cigarette lighters, plastic spoons, rocks, a bottle opener and other foreign objects. The current obstruction that had to be removed was a metal bedspring taken from the bunk in his cell; of course, he had deep psychological problems.

We have had inmates in the past who have swallowed balloons filled with heroin or cocaine. I remember praying for a prisoner who had ingested a balloon full of heroin. Unfortunately, he died due to the complications that ensued.

The following day the inmate who had to have the object removed asked to see me again. This gave me an opportunity to share Jesus with him. Having worked with inmates, I have learned how the mind of most institutionalized people works. He was trying to con me into making some phone calls and doing other seemingly innocent errands. I told him that anything I did for him was to be approved by the watch commander at the prison. We talked about his life and how he had progressed through the prison system. He related to me that at an early age he had been sent to the California Youth Authority and from there he had "graduated" to San Quentin. We conversed about what his own responsibility was concerning his actions. He considered himself a victim and claimed the state had violated his civil rights. As I was about to leave he asked me to pray for him.

As I left his bed-side I thought how sad it was that this 35 year-old would likely spend the rest of his life in a state run facility, being told when to eat, sleep, dress, and bathe. We have thousands of men and women who are behind guarded walls in steel cells whose only hope is that they may be freed from their self-imposed bondage. Paul the Apostle and Silas, his companion, while incarcerated in Phillippi were able to worship the Lord by singing spiritual songs. "But about midnight Paul and Silas were praying and singing hymns of praise to God, and the prisoners were listening to them" (Acts 16:25). I knew that if this man truly give his heart to Christ, he could experience freedom as Paul and Silas did.

As I left the room one of the officers stopped me and asked me why I wasted my time on "The Goat" (a name given him by the other inmates). Without hesitation I stated, "Because Jesus didn't give up on me." I am sure that I will see this man again, probably for the same reasons, but I will keep trying to share the love of Jesus Christ with him.

I can't count the times I have seen gunshot victims; mostly young men who have been shot in gang related incidents. Most of them are in life-threatening conditions. The most difficult times are when I have to meet with the family. The youngest gunshot victim I have ministered to was fifteen years of age, but most of them have been in their late teens or early twenties.

I may be asked to see a patient who is suicidal. This part of my duties is very heart breaking to me. Seeing young adults unable to cope with life. Youth in desperation wanting the pain to go away, a pain that is not physical but of the mind. For them the only way to cope with emotional pain is to "end it all," thus not having to face life and its trials.

The most heart-wrenching situations are infant deaths. They always leave me with feelings of complete inadequacy. There are several classes of infant deaths. They may die due to a miscarriage or perhaps premature labor and complications develop due to the age of the baby so that it can't survive outside the womb. Some mothers carry the baby to full term, but because the unbiblical cord is wrapped around the infant's throat, it is delivered still born. A rare few are born with a partial brain. I am comforted by God's word which states, "Then the dust will return to the earth as it was, and the spirit will return to God who gave it" (Ecc. 12:7).

The demise of an infant is generally the most traumatic for all health care workers. Dealing with the emotions of the mother and father is difficult. Each situation is different. There is no set formula in dealing with those who are grieving. Each individual will react to their loss and level of grief differently. My first response is to try to provide comfort in their time of need.

I have yet to meet a mother that did not feel some sort of guilt at the loss of her baby. They think they may have made some error during their pregnancy that caused the death of the baby. Perhaps they fear that God is punishing them for some past sin. For some, because they are not married, they feel that this is God's way of punishing them. A few feel guilt that they did not want the pregnancy and even had thoughts of aborting the baby. All of these feelings are real and, in most cases, are normal emotions associated with the grieving process.

Each individual has to work through the grief process and deal with their feelings. Crying, despair, rejection and anger may surface, but at some future date the pain will subside. When the pain is fresh it hurts so much that some even contemplate suicide. Only God can take away the pain, a process that takes time.

The Righteous Parish, and No Man Takes it to Heart

An example of expecting the unexpected happened while I was eating lunch in January of 1997. I received a page to go immediately to the emergency room. Arriving at the emergency room there was a "Code Blue" in progress. I noticed the concern on the doctors and nurses faces as they were frantically trying to save the life of a patient. Sensing the extreme tension in the room, I approached the gurney that was being wheeled to the intensive care unit. The nursing supervisor gave me a short briefing concerning the condition of the patient on the gurney.

The patient was a young girl believed to have been rescued from the surf at Big Sur, Ca. Little was known concerning the accident and why she had been brought to our hospital. The only information that we had on the girl was that she was a drowning victim. She had been air lifted by helicopter from the Big Sur beach area and a relative of the girl was in route to the hospital. They were taking the girl to the intensive care unit in order to place her on life support.

I proceeded to the intensive care unit and went directly to the room where they had the child. These were experts: trained to save lives, busy doing their jobs. I checked the girl's chart and discovered that she was listed as a "Jane Doe". I approached her bedside and taking her hand in mine started to pray. It was difficult for me to contain my emotions. I was weeping inside because I was praying for a child that I knew nothing about, fighting for her life.

As I held her hand the Lord revealed some things to me about the child. Because her hands were rough I got the impression that she loved the out doors, played hard at every thing she did, and liked doing things with her hands. All these thoughts raced through my mind as I prayed for God to spare her life.

I left her room and continued to pray silently for all those who were trying to save her life. They were preparing to airlift her to Stanford University Medical Facility. When I left the intensive care unit I felt that she would survive. I went back to finish my rounds, but little did I know how the life of this child would impact my life and the lives of those who worked hard to save her.

Later that day, after this very strenuous and emotionally draining experience, Tricia and I ate dinner and were about to drink a cup of coffee when my beeper went off. I called the hospital operator and she routed my call to the intensive care unit. The night supervisor asked if I could please come to the hospital. She told me it was regarding the young girl that had been pulled from the surf. I told the supervisor I would be there in a few minutes.

As I drove the two and a half miles to the hospital my thoughts drifted back to the child I had prayed for this morning, a youngster who I felt God would be merciful to and spare. I still did not know her name or the cause of the accident, or who her family members were. All these thoughts raced through my mind as I made my way through the streets of Salinas, and directly to the intensive care unit.

As I approached the girl's room one of the doctors caring for her filled me in as to her condition and her chances of survival. He stated that further tests showed that she had massive brain damage due to the lack of oxygen to the brain. He further stated that she could not live after the life supports were removed. The surviving members of the girls family had requested that life supports be pulled and had asked that I be there when she expired. I met the family of the young girl and offered my condolences and prayers. I read a few scriptures at the request of the family. By this time I knew the child's name and this made it much easier for me to pray for Kerry and the family.

The physician in charge of Kerry's care was asked by the ranking family member, to withdraw the life supports. Within a few minutes, her spirit departed from her body. Her life which would never fulfill its earthly potential had been snuffed out by a horrible drowning accident, yet she had changed every person involved with her care while she was fighting for her life.

I remembered a scripture that had comforted me when I had lost a dear friend. And shared it with the few family members present. "The righteous man perishes, and no one takes it to heart; And devout men are taken away, while no one understands. For the righteous man is taken away from evil" (Isa. 57:1). I believe that the Lord at times takes some of His creation from this world to save them from a life of hardship and extreme trials, which may be awaiting them.

This was a young girl that lived in a broken home with her mother and younger brother. Perhaps God spared her the suffering she would have endured in the future. I can only speculate as to why. I know her death was not in vain because of the impact on the lives that she touched while fighting for her life. No, her life was not wasted, but used of God to show us how precious life is to Him.

I cannot close the book on this calamity without filling in the pieces of this horrible scenario. Two other people had lost their lives while trying to save Kerry. Kerry's aunt was scheduled to run in the annual Big Sur Marathon and had promised to pay the expenses for Kerry, Kerry's mother, her little brother and her grandmother (also the aunt's mother), to come to California to see her run the "Big Sur Marathon."

Kerry had never seen the ocean yet was given permission by her mother to go swimming. Her mother was unaware of how treacherous this part of the ocean can be, especially for a novice. While her mother, brother, and grandmother were on the beach, Kerry ventured out into a treacherous tide. Her innocence gave her a sense of false security. Totally unaware of how violent the ocean can be, she was caught in a dangerous rip tide and tossed onto the rocks.

As Kerry struggled for her life, her mother saw that she was in serious trouble, and jumped into the raging waters in an effort to save her daughter, and then she found herself struggling for life. The grandmother saw what was happening to her child and granddaughter and she, too, without regard for her own life jumped into the raging surf and found herself battling the turbulent waters, only to lose her life in the process. Ultimately the power of the ocean with its churning waves took the lives of three generations, grandmother, mother and granddaughter, a tragedy that could have been avoided.

While this struggle for life was going on, a small boy of seven had witnessed the entire catastrophe being played out. He witnessed his family being decimated by the raging waters. I wondered what the young boy's thoughts were as he witnessed his mother; sister and grandmother, being tossed like rags in the raging waters of the Pacific Ocean? I was to find out later that night.

I spent the entire evening and late into the night talking with Kerry's aunt, uncle and great aunt. It was one of the most heart rending nights that I have ever had to endure.

Compassion at times is difficult to comprehend. This was one of those situations when all you do is simply be there for those who are grieving. The aunt felt responsible for the incident, because she had brought her family to Monterey. I was able to comfort her in a small way.

The one who seemed scarred for life and totally overwhelmed was the little boy. He will be haunted by what he saw at the ocean for the rest of his life. T.J. was the most affected by the death of all those whom he loved. I will never forget what he told me concerning the death of his loved ones. As he related to me the scene he saw from the shore, it was obvious that he was reliving the entire episode. He will relive this memory time and time again. His last remarks to me were, "You know what? I will never come back and see the ocean again. I don't like it." I felt like putting my arms around him and hugging him so that he would feel more comfort than pain. Only a loving God can ease the pain and in time completely heal him.

It was around midnight when I returned home from the hospital struggling with my feelings. I had been called to try and help bring comfort to a boy, a young woman, and a hospital staff whose emotions were tested to the limit.

I learned that when we walk in His authority in times of crisis we bring comfort to those who need it. When we invoke that name, a name that brings peace to difficult situations. "And the peace of God, which surpasses all comprehension, shall guard your hearts and your minds in Christ Jesus" (Phil. 4:7).

As I tossed and turned that night my thoughts were of the little boy. I knew that nothing I could say would ever bring back the lives of his loved ones. He will always be in my heart. I finally drifted off to sleep with the assurance that Christ is in control.

As a footnote on the events that transpired that day, first, I want to commend the doctors, the nurses and all the staff that participated in the life and death struggle of a ten-year old child. Each individual, that day learned that life is in the hands of an omnipotent God, though we must always try to save the lives of those in crisis. All of us realized how limited we were, a limit placed there by an unlimited God.

I close this chapter with a scripture that gives me comfort and strength: "Yet those who wait for the Lord, will gain new strength, They will mount up with wings like eagles, they will run and not get tired, they will walk and not become weary" (Isaiah 40:31).

Chapter Twelve

And The Spirit Will Return To God Who Gave It

The phone rings in the middle of the night and the operator asks if I can come to the labor and delivery unit. The voice on the line states, "We have a fetal demise situation (the death of an infant), Can you please come in." (I hate the term "fetal demise" used to describe the death of one of God's creations. It is such a cold unattached way to describe a human being.) As a Christian I believe that life begins at conception, but for the purpose of being medically correct I will use the term fetal where applicable.

I recall the first time I was called for a fetal demise. It was for a woman who had to have labor induced. During an ultrasound examination it was discovered that the baby was already dead in the mother's womb. A baby delivered at five months; is perfectly formed. I entered the room and was greeted by the mother who was holding her dead baby. This grieving mother was holding a baby that would never take its first breath. The mother asked me to bless the child. In order to bless the baby I had to hold it. It was an awkward moment for me for it was the first time I had ever held a premature baby. It was extremely difficult for me to hold back tears, but after I blessed the baby and baptized him as requested by the mother. I then turned my attention toward comforting her. We talked about the death of the baby and her feelings. She had a great outlook on life, but more importantly, she knew Christ as her personal Lord and Savior. Looking back I can truly see the hand of God in this crisis. Since then, I have held hundreds of little souls; most all of them have survived.

I prayed for the woman and asked God's blessings on her and her family. I left her room with mixed feelings, feelings of sadness but also feelings of hope and joy. A joy that this little soul that I had held in my hands had returned to the Lord.

On another occasion I received a late night call to go to the labor and delivery unit. In this particular case, all I knew about the circumstances was that the baby had been still born. When I arrived at the unit I inquired at the desk for more information on the demise of the baby. I was taken aback a little when I found out that the mother had delivered twins prematurely. The babies had suffocated in the womb and would have lived if the umbilical cord had not been wrapped around their necks.

I walked into the room and saw several people standing around the bed. A few were sitting. By the type of clothing they were wearing, the numerous tattoos, and the way they were talking, I surmised that the people I was dealing with were gang members, ex-convicts, or drug users. After introducing myself and offering my condolences on the demise of the twins, I asked to see the babies. The babies were both wrapped in blankets and at the request of the mother, I blessed and baptized the infants.

I wondered if the mother's lifestyle had been the cause of the premature death of the infants. I talked to the young woman about the father of the twins. The women told me they were not married, but that they were planning on getting married.

I cannot speak for God or play God, but the question needs to be raised, regarding His intervention in these matters. Did He allow this young woman to carry these babies to almost full term, then not allow them to live? Or was their death due to the lifestyle of the mother? I believe that we will never fully know the answer to this puzzle. Life and death in the scheme of God will always be a mystery for some. Those who live by faith in Christ will reap eternal life. For those who chose to deny Him will reap eternal damnation.

I cannot judge either the mother or father for procreating children without a commitment to God and His principles. But these are the people that Jesus died for so that they would have eternal life. I blessed the babies and prayed for peace in their lives.

As I drove home I recalled, that tears came into the eyes of the father, a man involved in a lifestyle that most abhor. This man lives by a strict code and one of the rules is, you do not cry. Crying is considered as a sign of weakness, yet in this moment of time, God reached out and touched his heart. For just a moment he cried. God had touched an emotion that was buried deep in the recesses of his soul. He was, for a moment a father, yet he was denied sharing the future with these two little lives.

There is so much we don't know about God when it comes to life and death. I want to believe that the death of these babies was a natural process, rather than a judgment. Scripture states that "there is no partiality with God" (Rom. 2:11).

Full of Grace and Truth

One Sunday afternoon Tricia and I were asked by one of the elders of our church to come to their home for a special luncheon. Shortly after we arrived at their home we sat down to relax with a cup of coffee. As I took the first sip my beeper sounded. I called the hospital and was asked by the hospital pediatrician if I could please come to the hospital. There was a crisis in the E.R.. The situation was very delicate concerning an infant that had been delivered at home that afternoon, and that the baby was not expected to live.

She stated that a young woman had given birth to a baby boy in her home while relieving herself. She panicked when she realized she had given birth to a baby. The young woman's parents were not aware that their daughter was pregnant. She was afraid to tell her parents. Being an oriental girl she came from a culture that could ostracize her for her indiscretion. The baby was in the emergency room of the hospital and I was asked to come and try to bring some peace to the crisis. I explained to the physician that I was in the town of Greenfield and that it would take around forty-five minutes to make the trip. She thanked me for promising to come and awaited my arrival. When I arrived I immediately went to the emergency room and met the physician who had called me. She led me to the room where they had placed the baby.

While driving from Greenfield to Salinas I expected the baby to be dead when I arrived, but this was not the case. Instead I saw a little baby boy fighting for his life. He was desperately trying to breathe, taking in large gulps of air. His lungs were full of water because he had been dropped into the toilet while being birthed. The girl had then panicked and hid the baby under a carpet. He had

93

been laid on the cold bathroom floor without any care and left to die.

The first prognosis was that the baby would be taken to a room and left alone to eventually expire, a process that generally takes a few minutes. The pediatrician made the right call and ordered the baby taken to the Natal Intensive Care Unit. Life saving measures were instituted to insure that the baby was given every opportunity to survive. The baby rallied after he was placed on life supports but was in critical condition. It was decided that he would be transported to the University of San Francisco medical facility.

I had many unanswered questions as I left the NICU unit. I made my way back to the emergency room area and went to speak with the young woman who had given birth to the little boy. When I entered the room there were two other women in the room with her. I introduced myself and explained my role in this scenario. They informed me regarding what had transpired earlier in the day concerning the birth of the baby.

The girl had gotten pregnant from a young man she had met at one of the local colleges. She claimed that she did not know that she was pregnant (I believe that she was too ashamed to tell her parents that she was pregnant), but that when she went to the bathroom to have a bowel movement the baby dropped into the toilet. She then hid him under a rug in the bathroom. She came out of her room screaming and crying. Her cousin heard her screaming and saw her bleeding and immediately drove her to the hospital. On the way to the hospital she told her cousin she had given birth to a baby. When they arrived at the hospital the cousin told the medical staff that the patient being admitted to N.M.C. had just given birth to a baby.

An ambulance was dispatched to the home of the girl and the paramedics rushed into the home, looking for the infant. The girl's parents, holding the dying infant in their arms confronted them. Because both parent's were non-English speaking the entire situation was extremely difficult. They quickly transported the infant to the hospital.

Whether the young woman knew she was pregnant or not, I cannot judge. She panicked when she gave birth. What went through her mind we can only speculate, but based on her cultural and racial background, and her state of mind, I suppose I can sympathize with her as to her actions. She made a decision that will haunt her for life. One thing is very clear she will have to live with the thought of that little infant boy, a baby who was conceived in a moment of passion. Unless they confess their sins and turn to Christ, she and the young man who fathered the child will have to face God for their actions. The child died a few days later in San Francisco. Everything that medical science could do was done for the infant, but in the end God took him home.

There were no criminal actions or charges filed by the Coroners office against the girl. They ruled that she acted in desperation and fright and felt that no criminal action was warranted. He ruled that due to the circumstances it would be difficult to prove intent, so the case was closed.

The girl was kept in the hospital for observation for a few days, which gave me an opportunity to converse with her a couple of times. She was remorseful and full of guilt when I met with her. It's easy for us to be moralistic, but just think of the emotions this young woman will wrestle with for the rest of her life, and all because of a moral indiscretion. Perhaps each time she sees a baby she will feel emotional pain, a reminder to her of her loss. Her family will never let her forget the "shame" she brought on them. Each time she wants to date a young man, she will feel guilt and shame as she recalls her ordeal. As for the young man, he most likely will never have to carry the shame or guilt, but he will somewhere in life reap what he sows.

To me the real victims are the children who are conceived through passion rather than in marriage. Recent national statistics state that 33% of all children born today in the United States are born illegitimate.

This story had a tragic ending due to the demise of the baby, but the circumstances could have been avoided with moral truth and integrity. The girl allowed me to pray for her and ask God to forgive her, and I believe God did, but as to what she learned from this ordeal in her life, only she can tell us.

Tragic as this story was, what can we learn from it? First and foremost, all life is sacred to God. Only He has the authority to terminate life, just as He alone has the right to prolong it. God is sovereign: He gives and takes away. Second, man can and should do everything within their known knowledge to try and save a life, not help destroy it. The third thing we can learn from this is, that grace must always be extended to those who error in their life. Only God has the right to condemn and if a person has sinned. Let God be God.

I remember the first time I saw an anencepholur baby. It is described as "Congenial absence of all or all major portions of the brain." I was stunned, almost in a state of shock, when I had to hold this little creature in my hands. Because of the nature of the deformity such infants survive for only a few minutes.

The mother of the infant was a girl of eighteen years of age. The baby was to be delivered by cesarean section. It is my understanding that this is the standard procedure in this type of pregnancy. I was asked to go into the operating room and bless and baptize the baby at the completion of the procedure. I was not prepared emotionally to deal with what I was about to experience visually and it's effect on me mentally, but God had chosen me to bring comfort to the birth mother and her family. The staff members also struggled with their feelings and emotions due to the infant's death.

These types of births are rare and can traumatize you if you are not used to seeing deformed babies. I had to deal with one other such birth. Infant deaths always leave me with an empty, haunting feeling. Yet I know that for God's own reason He takes them home. I am comforted that He is in control of all life.

There are other birth defects that have a devastating effect on expectant parents. One that is not uncommon, but never the less impacts the birth parents with deep feelings of guilt is a Downs Syndrome child. I can't count the times that I have had to console a mother who is having major emotional problems in accepting the child born with this condition. Feelings of guilt and rejection due to birth defects of infants are common. One of the most difficult times for me as a minister is dealing with a mother who has all these emotions tearing at her. She may feel self-blame and shame because her new baby is not normal by societal standards.

Only God knows why He allows the birth of these little ones and only He can reveal why. Our responsibility is to nurture and care for a Downs Syndrome child the same as we do for normal healthy infants. God does not punish us by genetic mutation, but He sees a greater picture of life. This is what I express to the mother that has given birth to a Downs Syndrome child that she should love her little baby all the more and because her baby is a special gift from God she should thank Him. "In everything give thanks; for this is God's will for you in Christ Jesus" (I Thess. 5:18). God's will is that we thank Him in the good times and in the adverse situations.

The Kingdom of Heaven Belongs to Such as These

The Natal Intensive Care Unit in the hospital is normally a busy place. The unit is preoccupied with care for the newborns. Care and concern is given for infants with breathing problems and other sicknesses fairly common in newborns. It is touching to see, nurses holding babies in their sensitive hands and talking to them as they shower love and care on the infants. In essence they are surrogate mothers. The care these babies receive is state of the art.

I deeply admire the nurses who work in this unit. They are dedicated, loving, caring people, with a special call who shower love on these babies. Some of these infants fighting for their lives are faced with problems that demand constant care. But the care they receive is always from the heart. I am proud of our unit and the health care professionals that work in it. They deserve all the accolades that we can bestow upon them.

Let the Marriage Bed be Undefiled

An incident that happened in the N.I.C.U. unit recently pointed out one of the problems our society faces because of the lack of morality, which has resulted in a rise of illegitimate births.

One morning as I walked into the N.I.C.U. I saw a young couple standing over an incubator. Next to them was a woman who looked to be in her early forties. As I approached, I noticed they were Latinos so I spoke to them in Spanish. I asked the girl her age and she replied that she was thirteen years old. The young man volunteered his age as fifteen.

The young man and girl were the proud parents of the baby in the incubator. I asked the girl if she knew the importance and responsibilities of raising this child. I told her that the little infant that she was soon going to take home with her would require all of her time, affection and attention, that this little baby was totally dependent on her for all of life's necessities. I told her that her baby was not a doll, which when she tired of playing with, she could give it away. She did not respond, but the grandmother did. The older woman was the young man's mother. She said that she would raise the child, and the boy claimed that the government would help them with welfare. He wanted to finish school since he was a sophomore in high school, and felt that his mother could help raise the child.

What transpired next shows what is wrong with some segments of our society. This "pillar of virtue", this "wonderful example of manhood," proudly announced that this baby was his second child, having fathered his first from another young woman. I was not shocked or surprised, but felt myself becoming angry at the audacity of this young sexual predator. Proudly announcing his virility to me he claimed that this baby was the result of one of his sexual encounters, and conquests.

The saddest part of this scenario was that his mother was affirming her son's promiscuity. I was wondering what had happened to statutory rape? What happened to parental control and guidance? At this point I excused myself and left the unit wondering about the plight of the baby and what lay in store for the girl. I knew in my heart what would happen to the young man; he, would most likely continue to have sex with many more unsuspecting vulnerable young women and never be held accountable for his actions.

A recent study on California Latino teens stated that between the ages of thirteen and seventeen years of age 92% of the babies born are illegitimate. The cruelest statistic also stated that after the first year 98% of the males desert the mother.

Let us not underestimate the gravity of the moral laxity in our society, with children birthing children. We need to address the real underlying issue for this in our society, the lack of parental responsibility for the actions of their children. We have a pandemic crisis in our country dealing with premarital sex among our young. Who is responsible for this crisis? I believe we all share a part of the guilt and shame. Parenting is a responsibility given by God. We will all be held accountable for the way we raise our children.

Secular society would label the young man and girl as victims. God specifically states that procreation should be between a married couple. Both of these young people will be held accountable for their sins, as well as the mother of the boy for not demanding a better standard for her son.

The idea that some have in our society is that if they have children out of wedlock the government will provide for the care and welfare of the infant. God's word is very clear about fornication but for too many of our young people being sexually active is a way of life. Most of them haven't a clue about the responsibility of being a parent. God has stated in His word, "for fornicators and adulterers God will judge" (Heb. 13:4b).

One might ask who is to shoulder the blame and the responsibility for immorality? Are we to blame the media and entertainment profession for what they produce passes for art? Do we blame our schools and our churches? I believe that the blame lies with the family. The lack of responsible parents is one of the major causes of the downfall of the sexual mores of our society. Parents must be held accountable for the actions of their children. Children should be taught morals and values in the home, but unfortunately God has no place in many of the lives and homes of our children.

Scripture states that Moses gave instructions to the people of Israel when they were about to cross the Jordan River into the land of Canaan. "Assemble the people, the men and the women and children and the alien who is in your town, in order that they may hear and learn and fear the Lord your God, and be careful to observe all the words of the law" (Deut. 31:12). It is the responsibility of all of us to obey God's word. We are to teach those who do not know God that He exists and holds us accountable for the way we raise our children. Man is to fear God, but if parents do not even know that He exists, how can our children fear Him? Morality must be taught to youth and children by their parents. As responsible parents we must be strong role models for our children if we are to restore morality to our society. If we fail, society as we know it will demise.

I have learned that regardless of the need of the infant I am praying for, prayer is vital to that child. When we pray for the care of His creation, God knows our hearts. At times He creates miracles to sustain a life that is struggling to live. His desire is that we pray for all of our children.

Chapter Thirteen

Who Heals All Your Diseases

One of the most pathetic scenes that I frequently encounter when I walk into a patient's room is to see a patient with acute liver failure, a condition, which is highly noticeable. The individual will have an enlarged stomach, the whites of their eyes will be yellow, and their skin will have a golden glow to it. You know instinctively that the patient's days are numbered. Generally this is a self-induced illness. The primary cause of liver failure is generally drug and alcohol abuse. There are other forms of liver failure, but most recently Hepatitis C is responsible for the rise of liver failure.

It is heart wrenching to see people with this illness because there is no known cure. Transplants are rare since they are based on the availability of a suitable donor. Unfortunately not everyone is a candidate for a transplant. Age and lifestyle are factors, which helps to determine as to who becomes a candidate for a transplant.

A famous baseball player, Mickey Mantle, was given a liver transplant, yet died a few months later due to the advanced stages of cancer. His disease was a result of his life style but he flirted with death all of his life because he abused alcohol.

I knew Mickey Mantle casually as a young man. We both played baseball in the minor leagues. He was playing for the New York Yankees farm team in Independence, Kansas, and I was with a Chicago Cubs farm team in Carthage, Missouri. We were both rookies at the same time. I never dreamed that he would achieve such notoriety as a professional athlete. I will always remember him as a great baseball player, but a tragic human being that allowed alcohol to dictate his life. I am saddened that his legacy as a great ball player was tarnished by his abuse of alcohol.

What makes it difficult for me, in trying to minister to those with this disease, is that most of them are in complete denial that they are terminal. I encounter people with this disease in large proportions in the Latino community. Many have asked why is alcoholism

101

so rampant in the Latino community. The answer is simple. Many in the Latino community introduce their children to alcohol at an early age. This has been a problem in the Latino community for many years.

Culture plays a very important role in the way we approach alcohol addiction. Education against the pitfalls of alcohol and what can happen to an individual is practically non-existent in the Latino community. Latino youths have a mindset that dictates, "If I want to be accepted by my peers, then I must consume alcohol."

I have painted a sad scenario of the abuses of alcohol and drugs and what addicts can expect. The most lamentable is when alcoholics are afflicted with liver disease; they seldom come to grips with its seriousness. Most remain in total denial, as to the hopelessness of their situation.

A case in point had to do with a man of fifty who was admitted to the hospital due to liver failure. As I entered his room his wife was sitting in a chair crying. She related to me that they were both Christians, but their marriage was shattered due to his drinking. Through his abuse of alcohol he had contacted Hepatitis C. She went on to tell me that they were separated due to his drinking which led to his abuse of her and their children. She had resolved to stay with him until his eminent demise. Doctors had given him a few days to live yet for some reason God prolonged his life. This tragic story was heart shattering, yet he reaped what he had sown. This man had been a professional golfer, but due to his addiction to alcohol, he squandered his money and died a pauper.

Billions of dollars have been spent over the years in the treatment of alcoholism. I have been involved with two patients who both spent over three months in the Intensive Care Unit with pancreas and liver problems due to alcohol abuse. The monetary resources that were spent on these patients, simply to keep them alive, ran into the millions. All this could have been avoided if their lifestyles had been different.

There are many other diseases that could be maintained to a bare minimum if humans would change their lifestyles. Some heart disease, diabetes, hypertension, are self-induced by poor eating habits, but can be controlled with proper healthy diets. Some are caused by genetic problems or birth defects but again can be controlled with medications and proper diets.

God wants us to be good stewards of our bodies. Paul writes, "Or do you not know that your body is a temple of the Holy Spirit who is in you, whom you have from God, and that you are not your own? For you have been bought with a price; therefore glorify God in your body" (1Cor. 6:19-20). As Christians we are admonished to be careful how we use our bodies. Proper foods and abstention from alcohol will in most cases keep your body in good health.

Suffer the Little Children

One of the most painful times for me is when a child dies. I answered a call to report to the ER to console the parent's of an eight-month old infant which, had died. When I arrived at the emergency room I was led to one of the private rooms to view the body. What I saw startled me leaving me numb for several days. I have seen hundreds of dead bodies over the years, but when you see a child or an infant it is much more painful.

Lying on the bed was an infant who was completely covered with red eruptions. The child had succumbed to chickenpox. It was one of the few times I have put on gloves to pray for a person. I did so because this virus is highly contagious.

What made this death more difficult to accept, was that the child would not have died if she had received proper care before she was brought to the hospital. We later learned that she had been treated at another facility and sent home. It is possible that the mother had used some unorthodox treatments and compounded the problem, thus causing the child's death.

I had been called to try to bring some comfort to the mother. I was asked to interpret for the physician because the mother could not speak English. By law a physician has to notify the next of kin about the death of a person. To make matters worse, the mother was also infected with the virus and was completely covered with the red eruptions. When we told the mother that her baby had died, I don't believe I have ever heard such cries of pain before. The anguish that this woman suffered was almost haunting. When the father arrived we had to go through the same cries of pain.

Everything: humanly possibly was done by the entire staff to save the life of this child. It was a total team effort. They have my greatest respect and admiration for how they performed their tasks in trying to save this precious child's life.

This story ended tragically with the death of the child, but I was reminded that medicine has many limitations. Unfortunately some segments of the general populace are ignorant of how to treat certain childhood diseases. If she had been vaccinated prior she would not have contacted the disease. Parents need to be well informed if they are going to raise children.

My heart ached over the death of this baby, a precious life that had been cut short. Jesus said, "Let the little children come to Me, and do not forbid them; for of such is the kingdom of God" (Matt. 19:14). The child who succumbed went to be with Jesus. Jesus in other passages speaks of His love for children. As parents and grandparents we must be constantly on guard for the protection of our children. "Train up a child in the way he should go, even when he is old he will not depart from it" (Prov. 22:6).

Chapter Fourteen

Reaping What We Sow

Much has been said and written about AIDS and how it is contacted and how it progresses. AIDS, "acquired immune deficiency syndrome" is predominantly found in homosexual males who practice anal intercourse and among drug addicts who share intravenous needles. There are others who have contacted this dreaded plague by blood transfusions and still others by a promiscuous heterosexual partner.

The disease goes through a progression that eventually incapacitates the person infected. As of this date there is no known cure for the disease. We must show compassion for those who contact this disease and pray that God will be merciful to any individual who is infected.

I have been asked to officiate at funerals for those who have died of AIDS and it is not an easy thing to do. Emotional pain and trauma are real in any death situation, regardless of how the individual expired. We must show compassion towards all.

Once I was asked to visit an AIDS patient at the hospital, a young woman who was in the final stages of the disease. It was a pitiful sight to see, a human being so emaciated, with most of her body covered with sores. Her mouth and nose were oozing blood and her life was ebbing away as she cried out in pain and anguish. How could anyone fail to have compassion? I was asked by the family to pray for her.

Her mother was a small elderly Asian woman who came over to where I was standing. She was weeping, totally distraught because of the condition of her daughter. She was imploring me, almost begging me, to intercede on her daughter's behalf to God, that God would somehow have mercy on her and create a miracle and spare her life. The mother did not say this in words, but it was clear by her actions. She grabbed my hand and started kissing it as she wept. I felt so inadequate as I placed my arm around her shoulder and let her weep. I was at a total loss for words of comfort, but it was one of those moments where just being there was enough to bring some comfort to this elderly woman.

The young woman passed away the next day. I was saddened by the incident as I reflected on the cause of her demise. She had contacted the dreaded disease due to her abuse of drugs and a promiscuous lifestyle. I knew God would be compassionate and if the woman repented she would have been forgiven. I do not know if she asked for forgiveness or if she was a believer. The day I saw her she was comatose and unable to respond to my prayers. It was one of those situations in which we must trust God for His mercy.

I have had other encounters with AIDS patients. Not all have been so traumatic as the one I just described. AIDS patients handle their illness differently, but all have one thing in common, the hope that science will find a cure for this scourge. I will always remember the little Asian woman who pleaded with me to implore God to heal her daughter. Due to her culture, she will undoubtedly bare the shame of her daughter's lifestyle and death to her grave.

Death by AIDS is a horrible way to die, but it can be avoided by a change of mankind's lifestyle. "For whatever a man sows, this he will also reap" (Gal. 6:7b).

When this country stops protecting a venereal disease and starts treating it as such, then we will be on the road to purging this evil from our society. AIDS has been politicized because of the pressure that has been placed on the politicians in Washington by a special interest group. Billions of dollars have been spent on research in order to find a cure, yet they will never find a cure, because AIDS is a virus. There is no known cure for any type of virus. Perhaps they will develop a vaccination to immunize people, so they can continue their aberrant lifestyles.

AIDS will continue to plague our society as long as certain segments of mankind continue to defy God by the life-styles they select. We are to be compassionate towards people regardless of their sexual preference or the color of their skin, or their religious beliefs, for we are His creation. Bigotry and intolerance does not have a place when ministering to people, who are ill or dying.

We are to be Christ-like in all we do. Like Jesus we are to be "full of grace and truth" (John 1:14c). God extends grace to all through His Son, our Lord and Savior. Grace is part of His character. If we love God, we will love His creation.

I was personally challenged by what I have just stated above a few years ago. I was on duty at the hospital and was asked by a man if I made house calls. My reply was, of course. He asked me if I would go to his mother's home and pray for a sick brother. I left the hospital and went to their home. When I arrived at the home, I was immediately taken to his room. When I entered his room I tried to converse with him, but because of the progression of his disease, he could not respond. He was showing signs of dementia that made it impossible for him to follow a conversation. Dementia is one of the characteristics of the final stages of AIDS. I prayed for him and anointed him with oil and then left.

The next time I saw him was at the hospital just before he expired. By this time I had established some rapport with his family, and was able to minister to them during his stay. When he passed away the family asked me to officiate at his funeral.

The funeral was extremely difficult for me due to the nature of his illness and some of those in attendance. I arrived at the mortuary and was greeted by one of the family members. I expressed my condolences and went into the sanctuary. The pews were full of family and friends. The front pew of the sanctuary was for the family of the deceased and close friends.

Some of the people who were sitting in the front row were homosexuals and lesbians. In my heart I felt saddened and pained for them as well. They were grieving the loss of a friend and brother. As human beings they have the same feelings, grief, sorrow, and emotional pain that others have. Weeping and sadness are emotions we all experience. Emotions affect all of us regardless of our sexual orientation and preference. The difference between them and others, is their choice of life style. All I saw was grieving people, men and woman crying and hurting, feeling the pain and the loss of a loved one.

As I stood at the podium my thoughts focused on how Jesus would minister to these hurting souls? I heard that little soft voice inside that said, "Love them as I do."

When I finished the services I walked over to two young women who were lesbians, who were deeply affected by the passing of their friend and brother, weeping and sobbing at their loss. I told them that they needed a hug and that it was all right to weep. I hugged them both and tried in my own way to comfort them. I remember that one of the young women broke and started sobbing as I spoke to her the love of Christ.

I was not there to judge their life-styles, only God has that right, but as I stated above, I was challenged by what God teaches in His word, "But now abide, faith, hope, love, these three; but the greatest of these is love" (I Cor. 13:13).

If I am to be a witness for Christ then His love must be the way I judge each situation, each circumstance. Judge the sin, but not the sinner. My message that day was one of hope in Christ, if we give our lives to Him. I said nothing to endorse their life styles, but assured them that God loves them and could take away their pain.

A final thought on AIDS: How we can help combat this dreaded disease. We need to stop glorifying celebrities as heroes who have contacted this disease because of their life styles. Sports celebrities and other stars are often held as role models and whenever one of these pseudo role models contacts the disease, they are treated as martyrs or icons, when in reality they most likely contacted the virus by their abusive life style and behavior. They need to be treated as they really are, people living life on the edge. Luminaries can make a difference if they will admit that they became infected by a deviant life style, and quit trying to be treated as victims. Many homosexuals have told me that they wished they had changed their lifestyle before they contacted the disease. Sadly, for them, it was too late.

Parents and clergy, schools, politicians and those of the medical profession must teach abstinence to our young, that homosexuality is wrong, that drugs and a promiscuous life of sex enhances your chances of contacting the disease. If these basic tenets will be followed we will be on the road of eradicating this scourge to mankind.

Chapter Fifteen

The Effective Prayer Of A Righteous Man

The number one cause of death in the United States is heart disease. Stroke related deaths are also high in this country. The chances for survival, or a high quality of life are at a minimum after a heart attack or stroke. The monetary costs create a burden that may leave them without funds and resources. The emotions that each family member will experience will take its toll. Feelings of despair and anxiety become the norm in their lives in the early stages of the disease.

A family faced with the decision of having to remove life support from a loved one experience deep emotional pain and guilt. They see their loved one hooked up to life support machines, intubated, IV tubes placed in the arms and hands. All they constantly think about is how the person they love is suffering pain. For the family members and relatives it can be very traumatizing.

Other thoughts run through their minds, such as, if they had gotten the individual to the hospital more quickly could they have spared them the ordeal. If the person has succumbed they wonder if they could have saved them by quicker actions on their part. These feelings of guilt are real and common to all in a crisis situation.

When I am called to bring comfort to the family members my first response is, get all the facts about the patient, either from the family or the patient's records. This allows me to minister to the family with some knowledge of their loved one's condition. I try to find out their religious beliefs as well. Then I ask them if they have a church or denominational preference, so that we can notify their parish priest or minister. Information is very helpful for me in helping the family members deal with their crisis.

Each member of the family will react in a different way to the crisis at hand. I have concluded that the best thing on my part when

I first become involved in a crisis situation with a family is explain to them what my role is at the hospital as the chaplain. I try to listen attentively to them and let each family member express their feelings. It is much easier to deal with a small family than with a larger one. One of the family members generally takes over and becomes the spoke's person for the entire family. It is essential that you deal with the specifics of the case. I always try to reinforce the doctor's prognosis so that the family is fully aware of what is going on. I advise them to ask questions of their doctor if they are not clear on what he has stated.

I generally will ask the family to come into the patient's room, while I pray for the patient. If the person if already dead then I will pray for God's grace and mercy on the family. I always try to pray, as the family would want me to pray, unless it goes against my theological beliefs, and the word of God.

I generally pray according to the scriptures. "Is anyone among you sick? Let him call for the elders of the church; and let them pray over him, anointing him with oil in the name of the Lord; and the prayer offered in faith will restore the one who is sick, and the Lord will raise him up, and if he has committed sins, they will be forgiven him" (James 5:14-15). Our responsibility is to pray for the sick or dying. This brings comfort, peace, and strength to the family and to all those who are involved in the care of the patient.

I have even baptized patients at the request of the patient or family. Some of those I have baptized had already expired. This request is generally from people who are Roman Catholics. These are rare occasions, which are usually in the middle of the night and the family priest or minister is not available. Most people who are in a crisis situation are extremely grateful that you will come to the hospital at night and pray for their loved one and offer comfort to the family.

The intensive care unit in a crisis situation is a busy place and, at times, can be hectic. I have the deepest respect and admiration for the doctors, nurses and staff who work in this traumatic environment. I have developed a strong rapport with all the staff in the intensive care unit. I hold them in high esteem because of their dedication to their profession, but also for their concern for the

110

needs of the patients and family. As the Hospital Chaplain I am part of the I.C.U. team and without their respect for me, I could not function accordingly.

I have become all things to all men

Once I was called by the hospital operator at the close of our Sunday church services and asked if I could come to the hospital. An elderly gentleman was brought to the hospital having suffered a massive heart attack and was not expected to live. His parish priest had been notified but, because it was Sunday morning, no one was available. The family asked if I would come and pray for him.

I went into the man's room and introduced myself and spoke some words of encouragement to his wife and other members of the family who were gathered in his room. I prayed and anointed the gentleman with oil, and spent some time with the family. The family had an advanced directive that evasive measures to save his life would not be exercised. This is called a DNR, do not resuscitate.

I told the family that I would look in on the patient the following day and pray for him. I returned to the hospital the next day and saw a few members of the man's family and spent some time with them.

The third day the man passed away. I remembered the last time I saw him that I had stood at his bedside and was amazed at his hands. His hands told me so much about his life. They were strong and heavily callused. My thoughts were; "Here was a man who had worked hard all his life with his hands. His hands depicted his strength, strength acquired by hard work."

My thoughts also reflected on how our Lord's hands must have been, hard and strong, a strength that only the years of a master craftsman working with His hands would develop, hands that were both strong and gentle, hands that touched tenderly those who were sick and suffering. I reflected on how He gently touched lepers, the blind and the sick. He said "You shall lay hands on the sick and they will recover" (Mark 16:18b). These thoughts raced through my mind as I prayed for this man.

A few days later I received a call from one of the funeral homes stating that the family had requested that I officiate at his funeral. I felt honored that I would be asked to do the services. During the memorial services, I used the illustration of the strength of the man's hands and how they had told me something about his life. After conversing with members of the family, they related to me how he was always building something with his hands, most of the time doing it for others. "He loved his neighbor as himself." I focused the message and the eulogy to relate to his friends and family on how he had used his talents to help others.

I was asked by the wife of the deceased to sing a song at the close of the services. The song was, "Holding My Savior's Hand," a song I first heard sung by the great spiritual singer Mahalia Jackson.

My purpose in relating this chronicle is to make two strong points. First, I don't believe that God care's who officiates at a person's funeral, but that His Son's name is invoked to bring comfort and peace to those who are grieving. The man came from an entirely different theological background than mine. Secondly, that a message of hope in the name of Jesus Christ is given and that through Him there is eternal salvation. Physical death is a given based on God's time plan for all of us, but He is concerned that we accept His Son as our personal Lord and Savior, because spiritual death is eternal.

Paul the Apostle said, "I have become all things to all men, that I may by all means save some. And I do all things for the sake of the gospel, that I may become a fellow partaker of it" (I Cor. 9:22b, 23). God showed me a great principle. When we see people in need, and hurting, we must not come to them representing a doctrine or a denomination, or any specific group; we must represent Jesus for we are His ambassadors and spokesmen.

Chapter Sixteen

Show Respect For The Elderly

One of the most overlooked segments of our society is our elderly, especially those who become incapacitated due to an illness. As we approach our golden years we are subject to illnesses that may leave us paralyzed, or debilitated due to a stroke or a heart attack. Our hospital has an extended care unit where we house such patients indefinitely. A few are short term, care patients who are recovering from surgery and they require minimum care. There is also a few that need physical therapies for various physical problems, due to having a hip replacement, or having to wait for a prosthesis.

A large percentage of our patients have Alzheimer's disease, a disease that now affects four million people a year. It is a disease for which there is no known cure. It is very difficult to minister to people who forget who you are the moment you turn around. They are more than childlike for children remember you from one moment to the next, not so with Alzheimer's. The tragedy of this disease is that it affects each individual differently. The younger you contact the disease, the more aggressive and debilitating it is. The saddest part of the disease is its effect on the spouse and other family members.

There are other diseases that are just as devastating to the recipient. One of them is Huntington's chorea. This disease is a genetic illness, in which there is a slow degenerative progression of the brain tissue, which leads to idiocy. The person with this disease will eventually loose all muscle control and the ability to speak or ambulate. Sadly, there is no known cure for this affliction. People who know that the disease runs in their family can be tested to see if they have the gene. It can be controlled only if the person who tests positive decides not to have children.

We also have cancer patients that are placed in the unit to live out their remaining days. Some times we have AIDS patients, but most of them are transferred to a Hospice care unit. All those who are hospitalized in this unit must meet certain criteria to qualify for hospitalization.

We had a patient whose name was Maria. This woman developed breast cancer in Mexico. She and her husband came to the United States to live, and while she was here the cancer resurfaced. She was admitted to the hospital and due to the metastasis of the cancer, the prognosis was not good. I was asked by one of the physicians to speak with her about her condition, and let her know that there was not much more that could be done.

My first encounter with the woman and her husband was shortly after they admitted her to the hospital. I developed a close relationship with her and her husband by sharing the love of Jesus with them. I would visit her and pray for her, always anointing her with oil at her request. She was later transferred to the extended care unit to live out the rest of her life. I continued to visit her and her husband, looking to God to do a miracle healing, a healing that never came.

Up to the moment she died she remained in complete denial that her condition was terminal. Her husband is to blame for he insisted that no one tell her she was terminal. She was never given an opportunity to prepare for her demise. I will never forget the day that she expired. I was called to the unit and was told that she was hemorrhaging and would soon expire. When I arrived at her room she was sitting in a chair, crying, "Please don't let me die." When she saw me, she said, "Please don't let me die," as if I could stop the hand of God. I told her that I would not leave her side. She died with me holding her hand, as she gasped for that last breath. I prayed for her, the staff, her husband, and others who had become close to her. As she slowly slipped away, I can still hear her cries, "Please save me, don't let me die."

We hear so much about dying with dignity. She died frightened robbing her of dying in grace and dignity. I don't believe that she was given an opportunity to meet the real Jesus. She placed her faith in me, rather than in Jesus Christ. I tried many times to witness to her. I shared scripture out of the epistle of John. "There is no fear in love; but perfect love casts out fear, because fear involves punishment, and the one who fears is not perfected in love" (1John 4:18). My only hope is that God was merciful to her.

What haunts me today is the fact that she felt that I could hold back death because I was a minister. This reminds me of how futile and insignificant I am in comparison to God's Omnipotence.

Our role as members of His Body is so limited when compared to His Omnipotence. He alone is God. I will never stop praying for the sick, the dying, and the emotionally disturbed, for all those who need a blessing from God. I will pray for salvation for those who are perishing that God will somehow penetrate the soul of a lost individual. I will give comfort and solace to those who have a need and will continue to pray for miracles, but it is up to a sovereign God to respond. Though we continue to pray, He responds according to His will. "The prayer offered in faith will restore the one who is sick" (James 5:15a).

Amazingly she lived fourteen months after she was given only a couple of months to live. I believe prayer kept her alive so long. I believe God allowed her to live over a year with her affliction in order for Him to do something in her life.

There are many traumatic incidents in the extended care unit. One was a recent incident of a young man who was brought to the unit to be rehabilitated while undergoing therapy. He had been shot nine times during a drug deal that went bad. He was very vocal about the incident and, in fact, he almost wore it as a badge.

The night he was shot I was called to the operating room to pray for him. They were not sure he would survive the operation. While he was undergoing surgery he was given 12 liters of blood. I went into the O.R and prayed for him after meeting with his family, and mother. His mother had aged beyond her years because of the pain and suffering her son had caused her. He had chosen a life of drugs and gangs. The family had moved to the Salinas Valley in order to get the son away from the influence of the gang and drug culture in Southern California, yet he chose to continue his self-destructive lifestyle.

Later, when he recovered enough to start therapy, we would talk about the things of God. He was a very lukewarm believer and could not fathom why God had intervened to save him. Drugs and how he could beat the system were all this young man had on his mind. He had been involved with several Christian ministries in the past, but he had slipped back into a world of crime. I never stopped talking to him about the love of Jesus.

The last time I saw him he was in the out patient clinic receiving therapy for his leg. I recently heard that he had been killed by rival gang members; if true, what a twist of fate, or of the hand of God? It would not surprise me if he were killed. I have no way of verifying this, but if true, then I am saddened and pained in my heart for the loss of a lost soul.

A woman of 32 years of age was brought to the unit for physical therapy because of multiple breaks in both of her legs and one arm. She had killed another women in a head on collision while under the influence of drugs. There was a warrant posted in her chart for a "no release." She was on hold for the police department, pending the on-going investigation. She would have to stand trial for vehicular manslaughter.

She had asked to see me, so I went to see her in hopes of sharing the love of Jesus with her. Her tale of self-destruction had started at an early age. Drugs and alcohol had become a way of life. She shared with me that she was a lesbian and could not trust men. She had been sexually abused: by a family member at an early age. She also confided in me that she had spent time in prison for another homicide.

She was trying to manipulate me to intercede for her when she went to court. She had learned over the years how to play others and use people for her own purposes. I recognized early on how manipulative she was. Her stay in the unit was not a welcome one. She was very abusive and non-compliant with the nurses and doctors. She was later transferred to the county jail to await her trial. She was later convicted for vehicular manslaughter and sent to prison.

I was never able to convince her to give her heart to Christ. Perhaps in prison she will come to grips with her life-style and seek God's grace.

These are the tragedies of our society. Young men and women while destroying their lives consider themselves victims, rather than being held accountable for their actions. Each one of us will be judged according to our action. "Each one of us shall give account of himself to God" (Rom. 14:12).

There have been a few instances of what I call miracles. A man was admitted to the unit with acute emphysema. He had requested to see a priest or minister. I went to his room and was saddened by what I saw and heard. He was gasping for every breath, even with an oxygen mask covering his face. Unable to sleep and knowing that he was dying; he asked for a Christian to come and minister some form of last rites. He wanted someone to pray with him and for him. I approached his bed, spoke with him, and recognized him as a patient I had previously seen. His breathing was so labored that I told him not to try and speak. I anointed him with oil and proceeded to rub his back, all the while praying that the Lord would miraculously heal him. I stayed with him until he dropped off to sleep and then left.

I returned the next day and noticed a marked improvement in his condition, though a few hours before he was not expected to live through the night. As I entered his room a broad smile crossed his face as he acknowledged me. We spoke awhile and during our conversation he asked me if I had a Bible. I gave him a Spanish Bible at his request and again prayed for him and left.

Today this man has recovered so that he is able to walk a few feet and is able to have long conversations. He still needs oxygen to help him breath and is mostly confined to a wheel chair, but I see God's grace in his life. His life that was spared; evidently, so that he would have ample time to accept Christ. He now gives God the credit for extending his life.

Jesus said that we were to "lay hands on the sick, and they would recover" (Mark 16:18b). The act of laying on of hands is a crucial part of ministering to the sick and dying. Many elderly people are starved for affection. A gentle touch is a way of indicating our care. How many times did the Master touch people when he healed them? Some were lepers who were starved for human contact. The law forbade a person to touch a person who was leprous. Jesus violated the law to show compassion. Are we not to do the same?

I have a deep respect for the entire staff that labor and work in this part of the hospital. They are highly dedicated and committed to their profession. Some patients can at times be abusive, due to their illness. Many patients are incontinent. This alone is extremely difficult for care-givers who have to change messy clothing. They must lift and care for patients that are confined to their beds. They work long hard hours and most of the time do work that most people would not do. I see the staff touching the patients because they care

Do You Wish to Get Well?

The staff is challenged daily by patients that have lost hope. One case in particular comes to mind of a woman who was extremely heavy. In fact, she weighed over five hundred and sixty pounds. She had been transported to the unit in a panel truck because she could not fit in a normal sized ambulance. A special lift and bed had to be rented in order to accommodate her. Special classes had to be conducted for the staff in order to learn how to use the special equipment. Due to her size and the nature of her illness extreme emotional stress was placed on the entire staff.

The cost to the hospital and the county was astronomical, a burden that could have been avoided if the patient had managed her life and eating habits. She was not a model patient by any standards. She was belligerent towards the staff, refusing to feed herself and demanding care that was not given to any of the other patients. She eventually went home only to die a short time later.

The few times that I came in contact with her were quite negative. She reminded me of the man at the pool of Siloam mentioned in the Gospel of John who was waiting for someone to help him into the water so that he could be healed. My heart ached that she would not see that most of her problems were self-inflicted. She believed that God was going to create a miracle, a miracle that never came. She confessed that she was a Christian and stated that she was very active in her local church. As a Christian she was not a very good witness.

What I saw was not faith, but presumption. We can never underestimate the power of God, but we must never presume that if we vocalize certain scriptures, like making a wish, God will respond. The words Jesus spoke to the man at the pool of Siloam should have stated this to this woman, "Arise take up your pallet and walk" (John 5:8). Jesus teaches that we need to take charge of our lives in every phase, even to what we eat, drink and the amount we consume. Our body is the temple of the Holy Spirit and, as such, we need to care for it. Christ told the man to take charge of his life.

I Desire Compassion, and Not Sacrifice

One of the greatest lessons in compassion that I have learned is that it applies to all ages, and especially to the elderly. Medicine has come a long way in prolonging life, but we must never lose our ability to comfort the elderly and the truly needy. Jesus said, "Truly I say to you, to the extent that you did it to one of these brothers of Mine, even the least of them, you did it to Me" (Matt. 25:40).

As we age most of us experience all sorts of illnesses and disease. How we manage our lives when we are young will, in the long run, determine and influence the degree that we become debilitated as we age. Medicine can prolong life to a point, but eventually we all reach the end of our life span. If we eat proper foods, exercise within our limits, and live a healthy, low stress life we have a better chance of living rich lives as God intended.

As I walk the halls of the E.C.U. I am amazed at the pain and suffering that has affected the patients in this unit. Amazed, because many of the afflicted and ravaged men and women's conditions could have been avoided if they had managed their lifestyles better.

I often ask myself how Jesus would have approached the patients in this unit. How much compassion and care would He have expressed to all the lame, paralyzed, amputees, those who are demented because of Alzheimers, men and women with AIDS? I believe, because of His love, He would heal them all. Because He is

119

God, and part of His essence is compassion. He would comfort and heal the sick, lame, and maimed. He is the Son of God and the scriptures speak of His love, His love for His creation.

Jesus said "Go and learn what this means, I desire compassion, and not sacrifice," (Matt. 9:13a,b). Compassion is learned by our involvement in the lives of others. Mercy is one of the gifts of the Spirit, but compassion is putting yourself in the place of the other person. You feel the pain they are feeling. You weep with them; you feel the rejection they feel.

Chapter Seventeen

They Will Lay Hands On The Sick And They Will Recover

Most people have a very shallow view about divine healing. Those who have a strong relationship with Christ have a better concept of divine healing. Their concepts on their beliefs in the authenticity of the Bible and their theological belief

I have found that those who embrace divine healing as a part of their theology and have a strong relationship with the Lord recover at a faster pace from surgery or an illness. Their outlook on life is more positive. Their faith in Christ is very important to them.

When we study how Jesus healed those with various diseases, we find that He always dealt with the emotions as well as the body. We often hear the expression, "a sound mind and a sound body." Scripture teaches this very principle. The Apostle John states, "Beloved, I pray that in all respects you may prosper and be in good health, just as your soul prospers" (III, John 2). The key word in this verse is "prosper," a Greek word that denotes physical and spiritual prosperity, (Vines Expository Dictionary).

People, who have a chronic illness and manifest the same symptoms constantly, have one element in common that negates their healing; they have a shallow relationship with God. A major percentage of the people who have a shallow belief in Christ focus on themselves and their illness rather than the one who can heal them, the Lord.

The emotional state of these individuals plays a very important role in their affliction. In many cases the illness is psychosomatic. A recent encounter with an inmate who was in the intensive care unit at our hospital is a good illustration. This young man was brought to the unit because of severe chest pains. All his symptoms showed that he was having a heart attack. He requested to see the hospital chaplain, so I was summoned to his room. I looked at his chart to see the preliminary diagnosis, so that I would have some idea of his problem and his background. I approached his bed and could see in his face that he was deeply troubled. After spending a few minutes with him in conversation, he shared with me that he had approximately eight months to serve on his sentence. He was also having an extremely difficult time in serving his sentence.

His medical problems were psychosomatic for there were no physiological abnormalities detected in him, based on all the tests that had been done for him. He had such a deep fear of having to go back to the institution. The volatility of the other inmates and whatever else, other anxieties and fears was truly bothering him, he chose not to share with me. I suspected that he might have been a sex offender, but I did not pursue my suspicions.

I shared with him how Paul the Apostle had been incarcerated so many times, yet was able to praise the Lord in every circumstance. I expressed to him that he could be a great witness while being incarcerated and that he should use the time to build his faith by developing a systematic study of the Bible. We had a word of prayer then I left.

I thought about the young man's state of mind. Many people are emotional cripples who develop every kind of illness that is psychosomatic. When a real sickness or disease afflicts them they are unable to cope with it. This young man had committed a crime but because of the severity of his crime, he would have to endure times of deep emotional stress as he served his sentence.

I often reflect on some of the people that Jesus encountered in His ministry and how He dealt with those who sought Him out. I am firmly convinced after many years of Bible study that Jesus dealt with the emotions before He addressed the physical.

Imagine how the man at the pool of Bethesda felt when Jesus pointed to the real problem in his life. His condition was brought on by sin in his life. Sin is an act of the will. The will of the person involves the emotions. The conscience comes into the equation and plays a vital part in the healing process. This man's conscience was part of his problem and Jesus confronted him concerning his sickness by commanding "Arise, take up your pallet, and walk" (John 5:8b). We do not know what grievous sin caused this man's illness, nor what it was that had afflicted him. Only Christ knew the root cause, and He addressed it when He told the man not to sin anymore. Jesus also told the man that unless he wanted some other sickness worse than the one he had been healed of, he needed to take charge of his life and not sin any more. He had been in this condition for "thirty-eight years" due to sin in his life.

Put yourself in this mans place. Imagine being unable to walk. The mental state of this man was fragmented to the point that he had lost all hope, yet Jesus healed him. The Lord later found him and said, "Behold, you have become well; do not sin anymore, so that nothing worse may befall you" (John 5:14b).

Sin is certainly not the root of all sickness, but in some cases it is brought on by our lifestyles. A sexually promiscuous lifestyle can and will endanger your health. You can become infected with any one of a number of sexually transmitted diseases. The abuse of legal or illegal drugs can and will effect your health resulting in possible liver damage. If you use injected type drugs you can contact Hepatitis, or AIDS, by using contaminated needles. These are just a few of the diseases that in the eyes of God are caused by sin. The disease is not the sin, but the way you contact the disease is.

The rational that drug addiction and alcohol abuse are an illness is in my judgement, ludicrous. No one ever forces an individual to drink or to use addictive drugs. When Jesus approached this man He was, in effect, saying to him, "You must manage your life and be responsible for your own actions." In essence He was telling the man that he was held accountable for his lifestyle. He did not condemn the man, but showed him that he had to commit his life to Him.

The woman who had a problem with blood flow is a great illustration regarding faith. She had spent all her life earnings having been to numerous physicians who could not help her. Jewish law had made her an outcast. She was unable to fellowship with other people of her religious beliefs. The Torah said she was unclean. Imagine yourself in her place. One can understand the pain and suffering that she experienced each day of her life. When she walked the streets of Jerusalem, she had to cry out as she approached others, "I am unclean."

Shunned by all her family, considered a sinner by Jewish law, emotionally distraught for twelve years, suddenly there was hope. She heard of a man called Jesus: and she searched Him out, and struggling through the huge crowds that surrounded the One who could heal her. She was probably thinking, "If I can just touch the hem of His garment, I can be made whole." As she touched His garment, shaking with fear, wanting desperately to be made whole, God had mercy on her and she was instantly healed.

Jesus searched her out and ministered to her by telling her, "Daughter, your faith has made you well; go in peace, and be healed of your affliction" (Mark 5:34). When Jesus said to her, "Go in peace," He was comforting her, building her confidence, telling her the ordeal was over. She was now restored to fellowship and worship with other Jews.

He addressed her as "daughter," Why? She was a daughter of Abraham but had been shunned by her own. Jesus came to restore God's chosen people. By His actions in front of the crowd He was saying to the masses that He alone could forgive, heal, and make people whole. He brought comfort and peace to a soul that was almost driven to madness. This is the comfort of God.

I have mentioned two great illustrations in the life of our Lord. Two encounters that dramatically changed the lives of two souls. The affect that these incidents had on the populace was dramatic to say the least. According to Jewish law, both these people were considered sinners. Jesus knew how the Jewish people felt about illness and diseases. When He healed people, He showed the masses that He was Lord of all.

When John the Apostle wrote, "be in good health, just as your soul prospers" (III John 2). He was dealing with the issue of the soul. When he wrote about the prosperity of the soul; he was expressing what he had learned from the Master. He was teaching the early Christians that prayer would strengthen their souls.

We are tripartite beings, body, soul and spirit. John the Apostle was stating a Biblical principle to the recipients of his small epistle. His prayer was that life's journey for the saints would be a healthy journey, a journey of both physical and spiritual health. This verse has been used and abused by well meaning Christians who read into it that the Apostle was praying solely for the wealth of the saints. I suppose your concept of prosperity plays an important role in the way you interpret this verse. As I have stated and reemphasize, the apostle John was stressing the importance of mental health.

Our prayer should always include the healthiness of the soul, (the mind, the emotions and the will). Time and again I see people who come forward for prayer whose emotional state is unhealthy because they neglect their prayer life. Unfortunately, many Christians spend little time in prayer and reading the word of God. This is soul food. As we need proper food as nourishment for our physical well being, we also need spiritual food for the well being of the soul.

Scripture states, "So faith comes from hearing and hearing by the word of Christ" (Rom. 10:17). Faith is at times very difficult to define when it comes to divine healing. "And without faith it is impossible to please Him, for he who comes to God must believe that He is, and that He is a rewarder of those who seek Him" (Heb. 11:6). As we examine these two verses of scripture we are given a small glimpse of the character of God. God is pleased when we exercise our belief in Him. This is what pleases Him, our belief that He is God and that He can heal.

How does He reward us? He has an eternal place reserved for us because we believed in His Son. This is saving faith, the faith that gives us an eternal home, paid for by Christ.

Healing faith is a gift from God. We are healed when He decides to heal, not when we exercise a word, but when we in faith ask the supreme, sovereign God to heal us. It is my emotional state, my soul that cries out to Almighty God to touch me with His healing virtue so that I can be whole. There are times when He heals instantly and there will be times when He allows us to go through the trial and the testing. He does not punish us for our lack of faith, but the trial is to test our faith. Peter states, "Beloved, do not be surprised at the fiery ordeal among you, which comes upon you for your testing, as though some strange thing were happening to you" (I Pet. 4:12). When going through a trial it feels as if everyone is against you, that even God has forsaken you. But it is your faith that will sustain you.

How we handle the trial and the test is based on how close we are to Christ. Jesus addressed this issue when He stated, "Come to Me, all who are weary and heavy laden, and I will give you rest. Take My yoke upon you and learn from Me, for I am gentle and humble in heart; and you shall find rest for your souls. For My yoke is easy and My load is light" (Matt. 11:28-30). Once again, we see the importance of placing our trust in Christ.

The Greek word "rest" that Jesus used in this verse is used twelve times in the New Testament and means rest in a physical sense; and as a transitive verb, it also means to calm, to comfort or to refresh. This is what learning to live in the comfort zone is all about. You cannot live in God's comfort zone unless you give your heart to Christ. He gives you comfort for your mind, your emotions, and your will, the soul.

Jesus was asked, "Teacher, which is the great commandment in the law?" Jesus answered, "You shall love the Lord your God with all your heart, and with all your soul, and with all your mind" (Matt. 22:37). According to this scripture, we can make a case that divine healing starts when we yield our entire being to God, by how much we love Him. We must love God all the time, not only when we obviously need Him, but each day of our lives. He must be the One we seek and worship. Our being depends on our relationship with Him. We learn to become intimate with Him when we seek Him daily, this is rest in Him, rest for our souls.

Divine healing is not based on how you feel or the nature of the illness or disease, but on the sovereignty of God. Our faith plays a very important role when we are going through a trial, but in the end we must place our faith in Him, and Him alone.

Chapter Eighteen

The Comfort Zone

I don't know anyone who desires to hear the bad news they have been diagnosed with an incurable disease — any number of the life threatening illnesses and diseases that plague mankind. Perhaps we are told that we need to have an operation to repair a torn ligament in a knee or that we need a hip replacement. You may have been told that your gallbladder needs to be removed by a simple operation. Maybe you have diabetes and have been told that you are at risk of loosing one of your feet due to the advancement of your disease. Perhaps you are told that a sonogram detected a lack of a heartbeat for your baby.

There are countless other types of trauma that we as humans must go through in this life. A child may die in a drowning accident. Your son or daughter may be killed in a car accident, or they experimented with drugs and accidentally overdosed.

Your daughter comes home and tells you she is pregnant, but refuses to tell you who the father is. She wants to keep the baby, and you say to yourself, "How can a fourteen year old child care for a baby?" All sorts of thoughts race through your mind. "How will we face our friends?" Imagine the shame of having to tell everyone your unwed child is soon going to give birth to a baby.

The phone rings in the middle of the night and it's the hospital telling you that your son was driving while intoxicated, was in an accident, and is in serious condition. You are asked to please come to the emergency room of the hospital. You get dressed in a state of numbness, not knowing what awaits you at the hospital. You think that perhaps he has a head injury, is in a coma, or worse, maybe dead and they wanted to spare you the truth until you arrive at the hospital to break the news to you.

All that I have described above is part of the process of life. None of us want to hear anything that disrupts our lives. We have become a nation of people that seem to believe that pain and sorrow always happens to someone else. We don't want any distractions to bring sorrow or pain. Our society has become accustomed to demanding instant ease of pain. We live in a world that cannot handle stress or trauma of any sort. We want instant stability in each and every circumstance. This is one of the reasons that drugs are so prevalent in society; they mask the emotions.

One of the problems is that we don't know how to deal with trauma or stress until we are placed in a position that brings us to the realities of life. Life has its peaks and valleys. Death comes when we least expect it. Accidents will disrupt our lives. Problems will arise that we will have difficulty dealing with, but as long as there is life on this planet, pain and suffering will prevail. There will be times when we will be tested to the limit and wonder if God has deserted us.

Does God measure our spiritually by how we handle adversity? I don't think so, but scripture teaches us that God allows us to go through trials to test our faith. We are told in the book of Hebrews that "it is impossible to please God without faith," so the trials we encounter in life are to test our faith. Shallow faith will cause a person to feel more pain, more emotional stress, and in fact in some cases people turn from God because they can't handle the pressure.

In all my years in dealing with people in times of extreme emotional pain, it amazes me how each person deals with their respective circumstances. Some handle adversity and trauma with a deep faith, always trusting in God for their deliverance from the trial. Others become totally dependent on medication to see them through their crisis, others become reliant on therapy to help them cope with their crisis. Most survive their respective trial, ordeal and trauma, but those who place their faith and trust in God recover at a much quicker pace.

The mind-set of today's secular society is that we are all victims. No one is expected to be accountable for there own actions. Thus when individuals are going through an ordeal in their lives, they consider themselves victims.

Several years ago we had a young couple in our congregation that I felt God had called into full time ministry. Early in their married life they had a tragic incident happen, the loss of their first child. Both drew closer to God, but they slowly drifted apart, because of their desire for the material things in life. They had two other children and moved from our area to another part of the state. We kept in touch over the years. They were like a son and daughter to us. Their daughter had a horrible accident and suffered the loss of one of her eyes. Ralph was hooked on prescription drugs, and to make matters worse, he was involved in an accident that took the life of another human being. He was not guilty, but this added to their woes. Instead of drawing closer to each other, they became more and more involved in pleasure and materialism. Eventually they separated and divorced. Both of their children are into worldly life styles. The entire family shattered beyond repair.

Where did they go wrong? Shallow faith destroyed their lives. They never allowed God to heal the hurts in their lives. They never learned to live in the comfort zone. They looked for the easy way out. Jesus said in the parable of the sower, "And the one on whom seed was sown among the thorns, this is the man who hears the word, and the worry of the world, and the deceitfulness of riches choke the word, and it becomes unfruitful," (Matt.13:22). This couple never came to the realization that God was their comfort zone. They looked for comfort in the material things in life rather than in the one who could bring them comfort: The Lord.

I still hear from them on occasion; but each time I see them, I am saddened that they still are searching for the easy life, rather that serving God to their potential. I still believe that they will serve God. They are like the story of the prodigal son in the Gospel of Luke. I have faith they will all be restored.

Why is there such a mind-set within society today, that we must label all trials we are exposed too, as victimization? I believe it relieves us of any and all responsibility and guilt. How are we who trust in the Lord for all our needs to live in this unholy climate?

Paul the Apostle gives us the answer when he writes, "For I have learned to be content in whatever circumstances I am"

(Phil. 4:11b). Does it not make sense that the more we suffer trials in this life, the more our faith is tested? Paul the Apostle was telling the church at Philippi that life is a process of peaks and valleys, trials and tribulations, but through all circumstances, Christ is with us. Paul could say, "I can do all things through Him who strengthens me" (Phil. 4:13).

Most of us would like to live our lives in a false comfort zone, never any trial or tribulation. We want everyday to be the same, never any stress or problems, almost like a recent movie called "The Stepford Wives." This movie portrayed the wives of the men as robotic, never having any problems, all living in a state of euphoria. I don't remember the outcome of the movie, but what a horrible world this would be if there were never any stress or pressure in life.

Many of today's families live this type of life by masking all their problems with prescription drugs. Prosac and Ritalan are the most widely used and over prescribed drugs in use today. The real problems are never addressed in the life of the user who becomes reliant on these drugs. Some become totally dependent and cannot function without this drug. Prosac's use was developed for people with mental and emotional illnesses. I am afraid that it has become a monster rather than serving its original intent. I do not advocate that it should not be used, but I am convinced that it is being over prescribed and that caution and concern by clinicians should be used when dispensing this drug.

Parents who have over active hyper children are demanding that doctors prescribe Ritalin for their children, not knowing the adverse affects that this drug has. Why is there such a great demand for prescription drugs? Because drugs give the user a false sense of security, a security that needs to be reinforced as it wears out. No stress, no trials, no pain, again "wanting to live in the false comfort zone." There are other drugs just as lethal and addictive, drugs that people seek to hide their fears and the realities of life.

We are living in a culture that wants instant gratification rather than trauma. Trauma is not part of our vocabulary until a real crisis occurs and affects us. I believe this is why such a large portion of our society is drug dependent on either prescription or illegal drugs.

Many people don't want to face reality until they wake up one day and realize they are addicted. One of the most pitiful sights to see is to see a person hooked on drugs. All they live for is the next high so that the realities of life can be avoided.

A great lesson I learned as a young man happened to me, during the Korean conflict. I, along with four thousand soldiers, was on an Army troop ship. We were being transported to Korea. I remember that about the third day out at sea the captain announced that we would be hitting the tail end of a typhoon. I still remember the name of the so-called tail end of the typhoon: Typhoon Ruth. The year was late 1950. The ship was about the size of two football fields. We were all packed in compartments like sardines. I remember the night it hit. I was in one of the top bunks in one of the ship's compartments. The bunks were stacked six high with barely enough room to turn over. If you tried to sit up you would hit your head on the bulkhead.

The next thing I remember I was lying on the floor of the ship along with a lot of other soldiers. The ship was rolling and turning, men having to grab onto rails or whatever was hooked to the walls of the ship. I remember making my way to the restroom at the rear of the ship. All the while the ship was rolling and pitching, then I would hear a horrible sound, as the ships propellers came out of the water. I have never heard such a sound. I remember how frightened I was and what a feeling of helplessness I had.

The stench was gagging to all of us. I have never seen so many sick and frightened men, not knowing if we were going to survive the ordeal. Every time the ship would pitch and roll you went sliding all over the floor. The only safe place was actually on deck, where you were protected from the poor souls who were having difficulty keeping any thing in their stomachs. They were unable to venture topside because of seasickness and the constant pitch and roll of the ship. With the ship's crew and the four thousand plus men there was probably a handful that had not gotten seasick. They had what is called in seaman terms "sea legs." Yours truly was one of them. The fear was plainly seen on the soldier's faces, along with the sailors. But we survived the ordeal.

The one thing that is so vivid in my mind today is that this large vessel full of men going to war, in fear because of the circumstances, being guided by a small rudder. More amazing to me was that the rudder was being guided and controlled by a small wheel. The entire ship was in the hands of the helmsman. The ship being steered at the direction of the captain of the ship, a course he had set to evade the brunt of the storm.

Those of us, who did not get sick adapted to the elements and placed our trust in the captain of the ship that we would survive the storm because of his expertise.

There were times when I thought the ship would roll over because all you could see was raging water, but I remember praying that if there really was a God, that He would please see us through this ordeal. I was not a believer at this time, but I believed if their was a God, He would guide the captain and the crew and all of us to safety.

I am reminded of Jonah and his ordeal in the raging ocean waters and how he was tossed overboard by the crew. Jonah learned a great lesson from God. You can't run or hide from Him.

It was a great learning experience for me. I had no clue as to what faith was all about, but I knew enough to pray to some God, I knew that others were praying and I believe He heard our prayers.

A great illustration that depict the ocean and its turbulence is when Jesus was in a boat with His disciples on the Sea of Galilee, a fresh water lake fed by the Jordan River. Our Lord was asleep, when all of a sudden the wind started to blow and huge waves started to fill the boat. The disciples become fearful and were afraid they would drown. They awake Jesus and said to Him, "Teacher, do you not care that we are perishing?" (Mark 4:38b). Jesus awoke and said to the elements, "Hush, be still." Of course the elements obeyed Him and the wind became still. He then proceeded to tell them, "Why are you so timid? How is it that you have no faith?" (Mark 4:39-40).

Many sermons have been preached about this incident in the life and ministry of our Lord, but what I want to focus on is His response to His disciples concerning fear and faith. Whatever circumstance; we are faced with in life, Jesus is always in our boat during the storms. Faith must become so real in our lives that we can know He is there in whatever trial we face. You may feel that you are drowning in your ordeal. Fear has robbed you of your faith. Just as the disciples cried out to Jesus in their despair, He may say to you, "Child, don't you know I am in the boat with you?" He is saying to us "Trust Me."

The incident that happened in my life as a youth became a seed of faith that would sprout up later in life. I am impressed with how God started dealing with me in a way that would see me through the trials I have faced as a Christian.

Life is like a ship in a storm. We get tossed back and forth and at times it seems that our ship will sink, but based on the construction of the ship and its design, the ship will prevail. The Captain is experienced and has been previously exposed to many critical situations. He depends on his training. He has attained his sea legs by his experience.

The Bible states "His divine power has granted to us everything pertaining to life and godliness" (II Pet. 1:3a). I am amazed that so many of us forget that He is Omnipotent. His divine power sees us through each crisis, each trauma, and every trial imaginable. I know in my own personal life that regardless of what happens to me, He will be with me.

Despair, sorrow and fear will affect all of us from time to time throughout our lives. It's when we recognize that Jesus will always comfort us in our afflictions and trials that we become mature. In times of trials; if we trust in Him and need comfort and place our trust in Him, then whatever happens in this life, we will be able to look back and tell others who are going through a test; that God will be faithful. We then will have become comforters: Paul wrote about God being the comforter. "Blessed be the God and Father of our Lord Jesus Christ, the Father of mercies and God of all comfort; who comforts us in all our affliction so that we may be able to comfort those who are in any affliction with the comfort with which we ourselves are comforted by God" (II Cor. 1:3-4).

Over the years I have studied this passage of scripture many times, but only in the last few years has it become clearer to me. The key to this passage is found further in the first chapter. Paul

133

states in verses 8-10, that he did not want the Corinthians to be uninformed of his trials and near death experiences. He stated that he put his trust in God for his deliverance. Based on Paul's personal experiences and trials, he reflects that we as Christians, are to share our burdens and problems with the Christian church. Verse eleven states, "You also joining in helping us through your prayers, that thanks may be given by many persons on our behalf for the favor bestowed upon us through the prayers of many." Paul is stating that the prayers of the saints delivered him from his near death experience. He was teaching them to continue to pray for all circumstances.

Living in the Comfort Zone

Learning to live in the comfort zone is attainable by developing our spiritual senses. We do this by a commitment to a life of prayer, meditation and the reading of God's word. The Holy Spirit guides our lives only when we yield our lives to Him. Through prayer and meditation we hear from God. A finely tuned automobile will only run when it has gas in the engine. Our lives are like an automobile in that we "turn on" and "tune into" God by reading God's word; but what makes our lives run well is communicating with God in prayer. A good illustration is this truth, the incarceration of Peter, found in the 12th chapter of Acts.

An angel of the Lord came and loosed Peter's chains during the middle of the night. Peter then proceeded to a certain home where believers were praying for him. The Christians thought he was an apparition, but then realized he was real. He had been incarcerated innocently as a victim of a mad king who was determined to do anything to eradicate the early church. Peter was set free because God had a plan for His church and in answer to saints that prayed for Peter's deliverance. God's plan for the church and for Peter was realized.

How do we attain a certain mindset that enables us to live in the "comfort zone?" One of the greatest hindrances in attaining the "comfort zone" lies in our attitudes. Our attitudes affect our emotional state especially when we are confronted with a crisis. Paul wrote, "Be anxious for nothing, but in everything by prayer and supplication with thanksgiving let your request be made known to God" (Phil.4:6).

Anxiety and stress are especially acute when we are faced with a crisis. Every person on earth will experience anxiety and stress in their life. How we as humans deal with pressure when we are confronted with a crisis is what will see us through the ordeal. We are allowed to go through trials and crises for the purpose of testing our faith. We can consider ourselves as victims or we can place our trust in God and believe that He is doing a good work in our lives.

"Living in the comfort zone" results from our ability to trust God no matter what the circumstances. Paul said, "For I have learned to be content in whatever circumstances I am" (Phil. 4:11). He learned to live in the comfort zone by the trials and the afflictions he had suffered for the furtherance of the Gospel.

Paul wrote, "Apart from such external things, there is the daily pressure upon me of concern for all the churches" (2Cor. 11:28). He had just listed all the trials and tribulations he had endured; yet his greatest concern was for the souls God had entrusted to him.

When Paul and Silas were incarcerated in Philippi they were singing songs of praise to God. They didn't know if they were to be incarcerated for life, executed or released. Yet he was able to trust in God for his frame of mind and his life. He writes, "Now I want you to know, brethren, that my circumstances have turned out for the greater progress of the gospel" (Phil. 1:12). Whatever his trial, Paul always felt that it was an opportunity to share Christ with his fellow man. He further states, "But that with boldness, Christ shall even now, as always, be exalted in my body, whether by life or death" (Phil. 1:20c). Paul trusted God regardless of his circumstances.

Many Christians struggle with this verse. "For to you it has been granted for Christ's sake, not only to believe in Him, but also to suffer for His sake" (Phil. 1:29). Unfortunately there are some that teach that we do not have to go through any trials or suffering in this life. They teach that Christ nailed all trials and tribulation to the cross, therefore we have evolved to a higher plane than our Christian ancestors have and this evolution has taken us beyond any and all afflictions. Therefore we should reject any sort of crisis or trial.

When Paul and Barnabas were visiting the believers, Luke states that they were, "Strengthening the souls of the disciples, encouraging them to continue the faith, and saying. 'Through many tribulations we must enter the kingdom of God" (Acts 14:22). This verse makes it very clear that we will all encounter various trials and tribulations in this life, but there is a crown that awaits us that far surpasses any and all afflictions, persecutions, trials, and sorrow in this life.

Human beings, as they experience conflict, trauma, and trials, learn that this is God's way of honing, molding, and shaping us to His image. God wants seasoned people who have learned to trust Him in all circumstances. James says, "Consider it all joy, my brethren, when you encounter various trials, knowing that the testing of your faith produces endurance, and let endurance have its perfect result, that you may be perfect and complete, lacking in nothing" (James 1:2-4). Godly endurance is what the Lord wants from us. Paul learned this valuable lesson in life.

I can say that I have learned to place my trust in Him by the trials and tribulations that I have encountered. What sustains me is my commitment to His word and its promises. I have learned to love His holy word, the Bible. It comforts me when I need comforting. It builds my faith when I need faith. It guides me when I need guidance. Above all: it describes who Christ is and how important He is to me in my daily walk.

Life is like a hurricane in that there is great turbulence in the storm, but calmness in the eye of the storm. In order for one to leave the eye of the storm you must go through the storm. When you come out of the storm you are prepared for the next one, because you are seasoned by having been there. Some hurricanes are harsher that others. Unfortunately we want to stay in the quite calmness of the eye. Sometimes we can stay in the eye of the storm for longer periods, but be prepared, assured there will be other storms.

We will experience rejection in life; we will have times when we feel loneliness. Even times of hopelessness, but we must always remember that our Lord is in the storm with us. He is the captain of life's ship and will "lead us beside still waters" (Ps. 23:2b.).

None of us know what is in store for us, but I am sure of one thing we will be tested. How we handle the test is important to God. If I can trust Him for my soul and spirit, then I should trust Him with my life. What we experience here on earth is in preparation for eternity.

Chapter Nineteen

Lord Teach Us To Pray

Why pray? Praying has baffled scholars for centuries. Mankind has sought an answer to this question for centuries. It is not an easy question to address. If God is all knowing why should I pray? One reason we pray is to know the will of God. We are made to communicate with God.

Prayer is a volitional act. When we pray we are expressing our deepest feelings and desires to a sovereign God. We are also expressing our faith and trust in God for guidance, for an answer to our petitions for healing or divine intervention in a crisis situation. The most important type of prayer is when our prayers are worship of God.

One of the most important aspects of being a believer is the development of a consistent prayer life. When souls are saved we often place them in a new believer's Bible class to learn their basic beliefs, yet in most cases we fail to teach them the importance of prayer in their lives from the onset. Unfortunately, we ministers at times leave it up to the individual to see the importance of prayer.

The disciples asked Jesus, "Lord, teach us to pray just as John also taught his disciples" (Luke 11:1a.). This shows the importance they placed on prayer. Jesus taught that they should pray a certain way. Unfortunately, the prayer He taught them has become, over the years, a repetitious form.

When Jesus was asked by His disciples to teach them to pray, He responded with the most famous prayer given in the Bible. We have come to call it "The Lord's Prayer," but it is in reality, The Disciple's Prayer for it asks for forgiveness of sin and our Lord was sinless. Christ gave this prayer as part of the Sermon on the Mount.

This passage of scripture gives us a set pattern, or formula, that is extremely important for our understanding of prayer. Jesus did not mean that this prayer should be a repetitive form, but the principles that are expressed in the passage should be employed in all prayer.

The first principle is found in verse six. "But when you pray, go into your inner room and when you have shut your door, pray to your Father who is in secret, and your Father who sees in secret will repay you." This is personal private prayer between you and the Father. It is important to the Father that you give Him your full attention. Personal prayer helps us believe that God will give us the answer.

The second principle deals with repetitive, formulated prayers. Some religions use incantations and involve the use of beads and trinkets. Repetitious prayers are meaningless to God. God wants us to pray in our own words with humbleness of heart. King David often prayed by writing personal letters to God. The Psalms contain a record of many of these prayers.

"Pray then, in this way; our Father Who art in heaven, Hallowed be Thy name, Thy kingdom come, Thy will be done on earth as it is in heaven." (vv 9,10). In our prayers we are to acknowledge God's holiness. When we make requests we must first submit to His will and His sovereignty. All prayer is to be directed to Him for God is a jealous God. In this prayer Jesus gives us a way to obey the first commandment. We are to hold God the Father in total reverence when we pray to Him. We are always in His presence, but during times of prayer we have a special fellowship with God in the "Holy of Holies."

"Give us this day our daily bread" (v. 11). This is the only reference to our material needs in this payer. But we should remember that our Lord referred to Himself as "The Bread of Life" when He said, "I Am the bread of life; he who comes to Me shall not hunger, and he who believes in Me shall never thirst" (John 6:35). Jesus also stated that we were not to worry about what we need to eat, drink, or wear, for that our Heavenly Father knows our daily needs and will sustain us.

"And forgive us our debts, as we also have forgiven our debtors" (v.12). Un-forgiveness hinders all our prayers to God. Jesus addressed the issue of unforgiveness further in this passage of scripture (v.v. 14,15). How sad to see people pray for a physical healing,

140

for restoration of relationships, or guidance for their lives, while failing to see that their prayers are hindered by their inability to forgive. "For if you forgive men for their transgressions, your heavenly Father will also forgive you. But if you do not forgive men, then your Father will not forgive your transgressions" (Matt. 6:14-15). We should forgive others their transgressions even as Jesus, while hanging on a cross, asked the Father to forgive those who crucified Him.

The next principle has to do with temptation. "And do not lead us into temptation, but deliver us from evil" (Matt. 6:13a.). God never tempts us. "Let no one say when he is tempted, I am being tempted by God; for God cannot be tempted by evil, and He Himself does not tempt anyone" (James 1:13). He allows us to exercise free will, but we are held accountable for our actions. We ask God for help in our daily lives and yield ourselves to Him. We are delivered from evil by being in Gods will.

James speaks about men's temptations. "But each one is tempted when he is carried away and enticed by his own lust, then when lust has conceived, it gives birth to sin; and when sin is accomplished, it brings forth death" (James 1:14-15). Temptation and lust if given into, can destroy the work of the Holy Spirit in the believer. Though temptations will come, James tells how to resist. "Submit therefore to God. Resist the devil and he will flee from you" (James 4:7).

The last principle has to do with the sovereignty of God. He alone is eternal, and is omnipotent. The prayer speaks of His Kingdom, where He alone rules. Jesus again was emphasizing the holiness and omnipotence of God. As His creation we are always to hold Him in awe and reverence.

God wants us to pray in faith, regardless of the circumstance, or the severity of the problem, even if it is a matter of life or death. God delights in hearing from us. We may not like the outcome of our prayers or the time it takes for God's response, but God wants us to pray in faith and trust in His wisdom for the outcome. "Trust in the Lord with all your heart. And do not lean on your own understanding. In all your ways acknowledge Him, and He will make your paths straight" (Proverbs 3:5-6). The outcome of our prayers brings us into a closer relationship with God. Christian maturity is a process. Our prayers help us attain maturity in Christ while enduring the trials of life.

I do not use a formula when praying for the sick, dying or those who are in crisis or trauma. I listen to hear the voice of the Holy Spirit. Whatever circumstances I encounter on any given day, I need to hear the voice of the Holy Spirit for guidance. There have been a few times when I have felt uncomfortable in praying for people. At times I have found myself not able to pray at all, but most of the time I seek God's guidance in how to pray for each occurrence. I never want to be hurried when I pray for people who are in a crisis situation.

I am often asked how to pray for guidance in certain life situations, such as having to make a decision to withdraw life support from a loved one. The effects are extremely difficult for the one who must make the final decision. Having to sit in on a conference with the family and physicians is very traumatic. It is sad to see the look on their faces as they are told that there is nothing more that medical science can do for their loved one. Before initial contact with the family I ask God for guidance. When I meet the family, I try to hear their hearts, identify with their feelings, and determine where they are emotionally and spiritually.

My initial contact with the family is the most crucial one. When they are in crisis and need comfort, they don't need another medical expert, but they do need someone to help them through the pain. I point them to the One who can comfort them, the Lord Jesus Christ. I pray corporately with them for God's peace and strength.

When a family is asked to withdraw life support from a loved one, emotions run rampant and sometimes people, who must take responsibility, feel guilty. A question asked frequently is what does God think about withdrawing life support? My answer generally is," If God desires a person to live even if we withdraw the life support, since He is still in charge of all life, the patient will live or die, according to His will."

Once I was called to pray for a sixty-five year old man with congestive heart failure. I arrived late at night at the Intensive Care

Unit and was met by the resident who had called for me. She briefed me on the patient's condition and said he would succumb within a few hours. As I approached his room I recognized him and remembered that I had prayed for him on several occasions. When I touched his arm he awoke and recognized me. He knew he was dying and asked me to call his family into the room for prayer. All life supports had been withdrawn earlier and his demise was eminent. The family came in and gathered around the bed. We prayed and read a few scriptures. I spent a while with the family trying to comfort them. I told them that if he were still alive in the morning I would look in on him.

The next morning I went to the Intensive Care Unit and inquired if this particular gentleman had expired. To my amazement, he not only was alive, but they were preparing to release him so he could go home. Does prayer work? I know it does. Was it my prayer or was it the family who believed? Did the patient have anything to do with his healing? I believe it was all of us, but it was God's will that he live until God called him home. This man had faith that God would raise him up, but he also gave God the glory that regardless of the outcome, he would trust in Him.

Death is not final for the believer. It's a journey into another dimension in God's kingdom. One of my favorite passages is found in the book of Romans. "For I am convinced that neither death, nor life, nor angels, nor principalities, nor things present, nor things to come, nor powers, nor height, nor depth, nor any other created thing shall be able to separate us from the love of God, which is in Christ Jesus our Lord" (Rom.8: 38-39). God's love is so engulfing that there is nothing that exists on earth or in heaven, even life or death itself, that can separate us from His love. These two verses express His love so dynamically that it astounds me that we sometimes doubt Him when facing death.

Faith is absolutely necessary if we are to understand and believe God for all our needs. God's sovereignty is revealed through His Son when we study His word. A life devoted to prayer and supplication. Prayer and the study of the scriptures are the most effective way of knowing the will of God for our lives. Paul states, "But the natural man does not accept the things of the Spirit of

God; for they are foolishness to him, and he cannot understand them, because they are spiritually appraised. But he who is spiritual appraises all things, yet he himself is appraised by no man" (1Cor.3:14-15). God reveals His will to those who are spiritual and live a life of faith. "But the righteous man shall live by faith" (Rom.1:17b).

We place our trust in people who have been trained for their specific vocation, but when it comes to trusting God we often waver in our faith. James talks about the prophet Elijah being a man of prayer. "Elijah was a man with a nature like ours, and he prayed earnestly that it might not rain; and it did not rain on the earth for three years and six months. And he prayed again, and the sky poured rain, and the earth produced its fruit" (James 5:17-18). "A nature like ours," refers amazingly enough, to Elijah's humanity as being like ours. He exercised his faith believing that God would answer his prayers, God did. We are encouraged to do the same.

Paul stated, "Be anxious for nothing, but in everything by prayer and supplication with thanksgiving let your requests be made known to God" (Phil. 4:6). Does prayer work? Yes, it is God's will that we communicate with him. Jesus made it possible for us to fellowship with the Father and this fellowship is sustained by a daily prayer life.

His Divine Power

Athletes are judged by their athletic achievements, which are based on how successful they are in their chosen profession. For example, if you are a track and field competitor you will be measured by the number of your wins and by the records you have attained. A Baseball player's ability; is measured by how well he hits, fields and throws the ball. Other sports competitors are judged according to the requirements of their specific sport, yet they all have the same goal-to win.

All athletes whether professional or amateur, must have one thing in common in order to succeed; they must maintain a strict rigid training schedule. This training schedule must be followed in order to excel in their respective sport. Talent alone is not enough

144

to sustain an athlete in a level of excellence. Excellence can only be attained and maintained at the price of a strict training regimen.

A principle called "The Law of Continuity" states, "A level once achieved cannot be sustained without continued effort." The physical body must be honed to its limit. Raw talent at times will succeed in winning, but greater competition, demands a higher intensity in training. Because all great athletes know this principle, they train harder to maintain a level of success.

Life's trials are like the life of an athlete in training. Man's training is based on life's trails as well as a dependence upon God. By our training we learn to trust in God. While athletes use coaches and trainers to improve their performance, we must place our trust in God as we go through tests and trials. Though we build our faith by reading and hearing His word. How we personally view our tests, and deal with them individually, determines if we attain victory over them. The Apostle Paul writes, "But we also glory in tribulations, knowing that tribulation produces perseverance; and perseverance, character, and character hope" (Rom. 5:3-4 NKJ). So that tribulations, trials, pain and emotional stress are meant to develop our Christian character. Our faith can be proven by each trial. The end result is, "Now hope does not disappoint" (Rom. 5:5a). The rest of that verse tells us it's because of God's love that we will not be disappointed. This is our hope. Christian character matters to God. He lets us go through trials and tribulations in order to develop our character.

I am amazed that some Christians feel that they can run their own lives and, consequently do things out of God's perfect will. Imagine an individual who decides to run a marathon race, but never trains or conditions themselves for this grueling race. When the race begins he soon realizes what a fool he was, because he was not conditioned for this race, he has to drop out. Life is like a marathon race and our endurance, comes from training to meet all the obstacles we will encounter in life.

God's perfect will for our lives is to do what His word commands. He gave us free will and because of our free will, we sometimes make poor judgements, yet because His love is unconditional, he allows us to exercise our free will. Faith and trials are part of

His will for our lives. There are many passages in Scripture that deals with His divine will. "And do not be conformed to this world, but be transformed by the renewing of your mind, that you may prove what the will of God is, that which is good and acceptable and perfect" (Rom. 12:2). The choices we make in life will affect how we handle the trials.

I have had numerous physical setbacks, but through them all I can see God's grace has always been with me. Each trauma and trial that I have experienced has drawn me closer to the Lord. At times I questioned God, wondering why I had to suffer stress and trauma? But I always found comfort in Him. I have learned to place my hope and trust in Him.

Once I was involved in three different life and death situations in one week. The first had to do with a young man who went into cardiac arrest in the Intensive Care Unit. A team of doctors and nurses frantically worked to revive him. I stood aside praying for the team of health professionals, asking God to give them the knowledge and strength to revive the man. Each time they used the electrical paddles you could see the man's body convulse. He was a huge man weighing well over four hundred pounds. As I continued praying, I could see the urgency on the faces of the people working to save his life, yet in the end I also saw the futility in their faces. Finally death won out, but what stayed with me and left me with a deeper respect for God's creation, was that He alone is sovereign when it comes to life and that there are some things in this life that will always be a mystery.

A few days later I was asked by one of the physicians to speak to a mother concerning the seriousness of the physical problems that her baby was born with. As I approached the infant's incubator I was taken back by what I saw. Here was a little baby, one day old, fighting for its life. The baby was being hooked up to special life support equipment in order to be transported to San Francisco University for further treatment. The baby had multiple physical problems. She was born with congestive heart problems that would have to be corrected by surgery. Her little feet were deformed and she was blind. All her physical problems were due to being born with extra chromosomes.

This child faced another problem if she lived, bonding to a mother who did not love her. The mother had rejected the infant refusing to hold and nurture her. I encouraged the mother to speak to the infant and let the baby know that she was there for her. As I spoke to the mother the infant made whimpering sounds as if she was in pain. The sounds she was making were due to the life supports that she was attached to.

After a length of time the mother returned to her room to prepare to go with the baby to San Francisco. I walked over to the nurse's station and placed my head in my hands and prayed, fighting to hold back the tears, tears of sadness at what God had allowed me to see and be part of. This was one of the few times that I have asked God to supernaturally intervene and take this baby home. I suppose it was selfish for me to pray this way, but I thought of the quality of life this little child would have in such a harsh world. Her family would reject her even if she survived. This baby would probably be a shame to the mother and the family. She would never know love. I knew it was wrong to pray this way, but I know that God forgave me for feeling so helpless, so distraught.

I thought about why God allowed deformed babies to come into the world and was reminded of what Jesus stated in the Gospel of John of a man born blind. His disciples asked Him a question concerning who had sinned, this man or his parents. The Jews believed infirmity was caused by sin and, therefore, his parents were to blame. (The Greek language in written form has no punctuation marks, thus the meaning makes a difference when we add punctuation's). Jesus answered, "Neither this man nor his parents sinned, But that the works of God should be reveled in him. I must work the works of Him who sent Me while it is day; the night is coming when no one can work" (John 9:3-4 NKJV). Of course the parents are sinners, we all are, but we are forgiven of our sins by the atoning blood of Jesus Christ. The baby like all of us are born with a sin nature because of Adam's sin. Our sins are forgiven when we ask Christ to come into our hearts and are washed by His blood.

The parents of the man born blind were sinners but this did not cause his blindness, as the infant with all the medical problems.

147

We still don't know why God allowed this child to be born, with all its physical ailments but we do know that God is merciful and compassionate and He alone gives life and has a plan for all of us.

The infant died while being transported to the University of San Francisco. I felt guilt and pain for the way I had prayed. This taught me a valuable lesson, that there will always be times when I will never fully know or understand God's plan for our lives. Of one thing I am convinced His love is eternal and finite. God showed me that this small infant with all her physical deformities was special to Him and that He loved her as He does all of His creation.

Fanny Crosby, who wrote over two thousand hymns, was blinded at the age of six months yet through her affliction she was able to glorify God her entire life. Her most widely sung hymn is "Blessed Assurance." Her love for God was so great that she memorized most of the Bible. Perhaps this little girl could have been another Fanny Crosby.

Not everything in this life is perfect, as we perceive it. All of us do not have the same athletic or musical abilities. Everybody is not the same height, weight, or color, nor do we all have the same mental capacities, but what we do have in common is that we were created in the image of God.

Since God is spirit it seems reasonable that the image we reflect should give testimony to His creation. We have the ability to laugh or cry, love, or hate, to feel emotional pain and we have the ability to exercise our wills. This is how God created us. He never looks at us as simply physical beings, for we are spiritual creatures. I allowed my compassion to rule my emotions when I first saw this little infant, rather than allowing the Spirit to guide me. I am to show compassion when needed, but I failed to see God's plan for this child or her family. I was allowed a small glimpse into the nature of God. I believe He wanted me to see this child, to experience compassion and frustration in this situation, but to know that ultimately He is still in control of man's destiny.

The third situation had to do with a terminal cancer patient. I had met this man about three years earlier when he was a long care patient in our extended care unit. He was a recovering alcoholic, trying to set his life in order. I became someone he could trust and was elated when he went home to start his new life.

A few months after he went home he was diagnosed with throat and esophageal cancer. I became close to him and his family, visiting him almost on a weekly basis and sharing the love of Jesus with him and his family. He had asked Christ to come into his heart during one of my visits. I felt sorry for him because his previous life style had shortened his life, yet joyous because he would have a permanent place in heaven. He died a few weeks after he went through surgery and radiation therapy.

All three of these incidents happened within the span of a few days. I was affected emotionally because of the pain associated with death and the futility of man in his quest for self-immortality "and the futility of it all." The frustrations that I felt were not because these people died, but because two of the deaths were self inflicted, based on their lifestyles. The infant's death was due to the abnormalities she was born with.

Both men were given the same opportunities during their lives to follow God or not. One of them made the correct choice prior to his demise. I don't know what decision the other man made, since I did not know him. The baby is with God based on scripture which states, "then the dust will return to the earth as it was, and the spirit will return to God who gave it" (Ecc. 12:7). When King David sinned against God in the act of adultery; God did not allow the baby to live but took him back, David lamented, "But now that he is dead, why should I fast? Can I bring him back again? I will go to him, but he will not return to me" (2Sam.12:23 NIV). These two verses give me hope and reassurance that the soul goes back to God. David's child was conceived in sin, but the soul of David's baby went back to God. I am comforted and my faith is strengthened by God's word, because I know in my heart, it is true. Christian character comes at a price, like the Law of Continuity. Our Christian character is formed daily by the trials we encounter in life.

Peter states, " His divine power has granted to us everything pertaining to life and godliness" (2Pet.1:3a.). Every circumstance in our lives has been allowed by God to produce godly character.

Whatever the circumstances He provides a way for us to prevail. In tribulation, crisis, temptation, death, He cares so much for us that He makes adequate provision for us in every circumstance.

He has given us the Holy Spirit to guide, empower and help us live disciplined lives. Jesus said, "But when He, the Spirit of truth, comes, he will guide you into all truth; " (John 16:13a). "But you shall receive power when the Holy Spirit has come upon you" (Acts 1:8a). God is always true to His word; our responsibility is to believe in Him, trust His word, and walk obediently before Him.

Final Thoughts

When I started to write this book it was my intent to express what I have learned from personal life experiences, from what I have observed and learned from others as they went through times of stress and trials. My ministry is helping those who are going through a crisis, or a life threatening circumstance, and also helping people go through the grieving process. So what I have written in this manuscript I have drawn from my own life experiences with hurting people as well as from The Word of God.

I do not believe we can have true compassion for others unless we have experienced our own trials. We can be sympathetic, we can see others in pain and feel sorry for them, but unless we go through emotional pain and stress ourselves, we will find it difficult to comfort other's.

Learning To Live In The Comfort Zone: taken from II Corinthians gives us insight into true compassion. Paul writes; "Blessed be the God and Father of our Lord Jesus Christ, the Father of mercies and God of all comfort; who comforts us, in all our affliction so that we may be able to comfort those who are in any affliction, with the comfort with which we are comforted by God" (II Cor. 1:3). This scripture clearly states that God initiates the comfort in all our lives, because of His mercy. He uses those who have been through some sort of affliction as His vessels to comfort others. Paul states that they were afflicted to the point of death, but he thanked God that He had placed him in this position so that he

150

could impart this spiritual wisdom to the Christian believers in Corinth.

The hardest thing most of us will face in life is placing our trust in God when we are stretched to the breaking point. I believe God called me to this ministry because I was willing to serve and was given a special gift. This ministry at times frays your emotions, causes emotional pain, and frustration. This is caused by what you see other human beings going through. It is not a ministry that brings notoriety or great accolades. It seldom brings joy or happiness. Why do I allow myself to go through the stress and pressure? I do it because God loves me and in return I love my Lord and His creation. Since He called me to this ministry, I want to be obedient to Him.

Being a pastor and chaplain at the same time can be hectic, but very rewarding. I am fulfilled in knowing that people have been ministered to who may never set foot inside of a church. The babies I have prayed for have brought joy and blessing to me. Some of the employees have asked me to officiate at their weddings. Some call me to pray for them because they do not have a home church. I have been asked to officiate at funerals by family members of a loved one who has expired and have had the opportunity to invoke the name of Jesus Christ on each and everyone, of these occasions.

I have a little saying that I use a lot in my sermons and teaching. God has called us to be "soldiers of faith, messengers of hope, and ambassadors of love." If I can give others hope by my faith in Christ, if I can share with them His love, then I am richly rewarded, because He alone gets the glory.

Paul the apostle suffered and endured many trials and tribulations. He made a statement that has helped me to focus on what makes it possible for God to use us. Paul states "For I have learned to be content in whatever circumstance I am" (Phil. 4:11b). Life is a continual learning process. No matter what we encounter in life we will learn lessons that will make us into better human beings and enable us to serve God better. I am learning to place my total trust in Him.

May God grant you serenity in times of despair and hope in times of loss: I pray that you will never doubt the reality of His great love even when love seems to be only a word, even when you feel that He is far away. "Now may our Lord Jesus Christ Himself and God our Father, who has loved us and given us <u>eternal comfort</u> and good hope by grace, <u>comfort and strengthen your hearts</u> in every good work and word" (II Thess. 2:16-17). Amen!

CPSIA information can be obtained
at www.ICGtesting.com
Printed in the USA
FSHW021345070420
68908FS